Playing for Range

PLAYING FOR RANGERS NO 17

Edited by Ken Gallacher

Stanley Paul

London Melbourne Sydney Auckland Johannesburg

Stanley Paul & Co. Ltd

An imprint of Century Hutchinson Ltd

62-65 Chandos Place, London WC2N 4NW

Century Hutchinson Publishing Group (Australia) Pty Ltd
16-22 Church Street, Hawthorn, Melbourne, Victoria 3122

Century Hutchingson Group (NZ) Ltd
32-34 View Road, PO Box 40-086, Glenfield, Auckland 10

Century Hutchinson Group (SA) Pty Ltd
PO Box 337, Bergvlei 2012, South Africa

First Published 1985
© Stanley Paul & Co. Ltd 1985

Set in Linotron Baskerville
by Input Typesetting Ltd, London
Printed and bound in Great Britain by Anchor Brendon Ltd,
Tiptree, Essex

British Library Cataloguing in Publication Data

1. Rangers Football Club – Periodicals
I. Gallacher, Ken
796.334'63'0941443 GV943.6.R3

ISBN 0 09 162301 4

Black and white photographs by courtesy of Sportapics
Colour photographs by Sportapics and Colorsport

Frontispiece: Anxiety is mirrored on the face of Dave McKinnon as
he marshals his defence in one of the four Old Firm clashes of last
season

CONTENTS

ONE CUP SAVED THE SEASON...

When Rangers' captain Craig Paterson accepted the League Cup – and the sponsors' own Skol Cup – at Hampden at the end of October, everything looked good for Rangers.

And less than two weeks later, when a storming display almost sent Inter Milan back to Italy and OUT of the UEFA Cup, Jock Wallace's team appeared to be on the road to the success that the big man wants for them.

The hiccups which had interrupted the previous season, the slips which had marred their Premier League performances even up until that time, looked as if they would fade into the past.

Indeed the stage looked set for a battle royal at the top of the Premier League between the champions Aberdeen and the rival members of Scottish soccer's Old Firm, Celtic and Rangers.

It seemed as if the Ibrox men had found the form which had eluded them too often in the past. The way they had beaten the tactically aware Dundee United team at Hampden . . . the way they had beaten Inter Milan and embarrassed the arrogant Italians . . . the way that the players had approached these two games gave their fans the promise of great things for the future.

Then, again, the stuttering uncertainty of the League performances started to creep in. Following that Hampden final when close to 45,000 fans celebrated their second successive win in the tournament the team had a home game at Ibrox against United's city neighbours, Dundee. A dismal 0–0 draw was the result. The following week they travelled to Easter Road to face up to Hibs – and the result was another draw. This time it was 2–2, but after the glorious result against Inter Milan it was another disappointment – and another lost point.

The next week saw a crunch game at home and 34,000 fans were in Ibrox to see the champions, Aberdeen. Again, Rangers

The tensions of a Premier League season are captured during Old Firm clashes. Here Davie Cooper tries to break clear of Mark Reid, now with Charlton, during the 1–1 draw at Celtic Park a few days before Christmas failed. Earlier at Pittodrie they had gained a creditable draw. Now at home they slumped to a 2–1 defeat and eventually when it came to New Year's Day and the Old Firm clash it was a make or break situation.

If Rangers had won that day then they would have remained in a challenging position. And buoyed up by that success they might have changed the complexion of the remainder of their dismal season. But they failed. In the one game which saw a clear cut result in the four clashes between the great Glasgow rivals, Rangers went down 2–1.

Davie Cooper scored for Rangers and for a spell it looked as if they might win the game which turned out to be arguably the most important they faced during the whole League programme. But goals from Mo Johnston and Brian McClair made sure that Celtic, not Rangers, would be the team to challenge Aberdeen over the gruelling last stages of the Top Ten race.

More Old Firm drama as Ally Dawson, the Rangers full back, is ordered off by referee Bob Valentine after a clash with Mo Johnston in the end-of-season game at Parkhead

Finally, after being in third place for most of the season, the slump which followed the Celtic defeat saw Rangers drop back behind Dundee United. The Tannadice team, Rangers' victims in the Skol Cup, gained some revenge by taking third spot in the League even though, over the season, in the games between the two Rangers came off best. The Ibrox men beat United three times, twice in the League and once in that Skol Cup final, and drew with them twice. That was better than Aberdeen could manage. The champions lost twice to Jim McLean's team, and beat them twice, in the League, but lost out in the semi-final of the Scottish Cup.

But in the four games against Aberdeen, Rangers could muster just a single point – from that early season draw against Alex Ferguson's team at Pittodrie.

Even against Celtic, Rangers almost held their own. Three draws and that one defeat was their record there . . . but the

Disappointment here for the Rangers defence as a header from Aberdeen's Billy Stark beats Peter McCloy and defender Dave McKinnon to cross the line. Aberdeen won the Ibrox clash 2–1

More from the Aberdeen defeat – this time Rangers are on the attack as Neale Cooper tries to close in on striker Dave Mitchell

cruel story of their clashes with Aberdeen reflects where they were going astray. Even sharing the eight points would have pegged back the Dons and given Rangers a better chance of catching them. But one embarrassing defeat at Pittodrie when they slumped 5–1 was the low point of the season for Wallace and his players.

The battles with Celtic remain the biggest crowd-pullers but unlike the old days the title is not decided on which of the two teams do best in these games. The newer challenge of Aberdeen and Dundee United has made sure of that in the past few years.

So Rangers must lay the bogey of Aberdeen, plus they must lose the habit of dropping vital points to lesser teams at their own magnificent Ibrox stadium if they are to be the power in the Premier League that they want to be.

The Scottish Cup arrived in the ice and snow of January when the journey to Cappielow to play Morton was a dangerous assignment.

The pitch was bad and Rangers protested to the match referee, but the Cup tie went on and, in the end, plucky little Morton, set to be relegated at the end of the season, forced a draw. That gave them a money-spinning Ibrox replay which Rangers duly won and now they marched on to the next round and a game against more Premier League opposition in Dundee.

This was the team which had beaten Rangers in the same tournament a year earlier – and the jinx was still on. Twenty thousand Ibrox fans saw the Dens Park team win 1–0 with a goal from their midfield man John Brown and Rangers were knocked out of the only remaining tournament where they could make any kind of impact . . . .

That afternoon of 16 February saw the virtual end of the season for the Ibrox men. They did manage to raise their game enough in the closing stages of the season to defeat Dundee United at Tannadice and to gain a battling draw with Celtic at Parkhead. But, in the end, the one consolation was that Skol Cup win.

The sight of the two trophies sitting proudly in the Ibrox Trophy Room spelled out that the season had not been the disaster some tried to paint it.

That heartening Hampden win gives hope for the future. The three domestic trophies were shared out one apiece to Aberdeen (Premier League championship), Celtic (Scottish Cup) and

A jumping Ted McMinn and team-mate Ian Redford have the Celtic defence in trouble at Celtic Park

Joy for Rangers this time as Davie Cooper (*left*) watches his shot beat Pat Bonner, Brian McClair and Murdo MacLeod to give Rangers a 1–1 draw in the Premier League clash at Parkhead

Rangers (League Cup). That in itself proves how challenging the game has become in Scotland.

Jock Wallace has maintained that there are no easy games left in the Top Ten, and that the consistency of performance there makes it one of the toughest leagues in the whole of Europe. To win one trophy may not satisfy the hunger of the Rangers support but in light of the ever-growing challenges it remains an achievement to be proud of.

Not that Wallace will be satisfied with winning the same trophy twice in the two years he has been back in the manager's office at Ibrox. He wants bigger prizes, more important prizes and he wants a team of his own making to win them.

WILLIE THORNTON ~ FIFTY YEARS A RANGER

It was back in 1936 that the teenager from the mining village of Winchburgh first met the legendary manager of Rangers, Bill Struth. . . .

And it was Struth who had more influence on Willie Thornton's life than anyone else. Even now as Thornton, reckoned to be one of the greatest centre forwards ever seen at Ibrox, looks back down the years, his lasting respect for Struth is evident.

As with most players of his generation Thornton went in awe of the man who governed Rangers for more than three decades. 'No one will ever have as much influence on as many generations of players as he did,' says Thornton. 'And no one will ever have as much influence on one club either. He ruled Rangers from 1921 until 1954 and that is the kind of span that no one ever has now. The game has changed, the demands are greater, the pressures enormous, and it is inconceivable to think of anyone remaining in command of a club for more than thirty years. But Bill Struth did and he made Rangers the great club they are today.'

Yet Thornton, who became a manager himself with Dundee and then Partick Thistle when his playing days with Rangers ended just as the Struth era itself was drawing to its success-packed close, was talking about a man who never talked tactics. A man who had never played football, knew little or nothing about the finer points of the game and yet could dominate players who captained their country and their club.

Recalls Thornton: 'It was strange when you look at how the game is set up these days. But, at that time, we never gave it a thought. He never once discussed tactics because, quite simply, he didn't know anything about them.

'His way was to allow the senior players to decide on the approach the team would take for each game. And who is to say he was wrong. It was successful all the years I was in the team and they stretched from before the war until just before his reign as manager ended.

'It wasn't his knowledge of the game which counted – it was his knowledge of men. He knew how to handle men. That was his greatest asset. He was a very strict disciplinarian and he earned the respect of every one of the players.

'He had tremendous presence. You knew the moment he walked into any room that he had arrived. You didn't have to turn your head to see if he was there. I've talked about that with other players and they all felt the same way. There was something about the man, something which MADE people respect him.

'He was always remarkably well dressed, you know. He had a position as manager of Rangers and he lived up to that and he expected us to live up to it as well. We were Rangers players and as such we had to dress well too. Whether it was for training or not we still had to look the part when we arrived at Ibrox. If not then we knew we would be in trouble. On match days, too, you had to be turned out properly. He wouldn't have it any other way at all.

'Essentially, though, he was a fair man. You could have complaints now and again but in your heart you knew that Struth was always fair. He made the Rangers Football Club.

'Willie Waddell was the closest to Bill Struth in the way he managed the club. Willie is my oldest friend in the game and he modelled himself on the Old Man. There were many things about him which brought back memories of the days when we were players under Bill Struth. . . .'

Playing days started for Willie Thornton when he was just sixteen years old and his father, who never saw him play, took him to Ibrox for a meeting with the Rangers manager.

'There were only about three cars in the whole of Winchburgh at that time,' recalls Thornton. 'Yet we managed to borrow one and a friend from the village drove us up to Glasgow. I'll never forget that day. After we had settled my future – and there was no place else I had ever wanted to go – Mr Struth told my father and I that we should drive down to Clydebank before going home and take a look at the new ship they were building. "Don't miss this chance," he told us, "to see one of the greatest ships which will ever be built."

'Sure enough we went down there and No 534 was standing in the stocks where work had not long started on her. That was the ship which was destined to become the Queen Mary and many years later I was to sail to the United States on her as part of a Scotland touring team.'

That trip took place in 1949. Thornton had been a reserve at Wembley as Scotland notched a famous victory over the English.

Billy Houliston had taken his place at centre forward that afternoon – but Thornton shared in the special bonus.

He explains: 'I was one of the reserves at Wembley that day but, of course, that was long before substitutes were allowed so the players who had been named as reserves didn't even strip. We sat out there on the bench in our civvies. Anyhow, Sir George Graham who was secretary of the Scottish Football Association, had told all the players before the game that if they won then he would take us all on a tour of the United States. That was quite a thing in those days – we're talking about thirty-five years ago now – and true enough after the victory he did take us over to the States. That's how I came to travel on the Queen Mary, the ship I'd seen being built before the War, the ship that Bill Struth had told me to go and take a look at.

'I think about that often. It's almost as if he was telling me that coming to Rangers opened up new worlds. Of course, he was right.'

One time Rangers star centre forward and then the club's assistant manager – Willie Thornton

When Thornton came into the Rangers team at the tail end of the thirties he joined an illustrious group. There were powerful personalities scattered through the Ibrox dressing rooms – men who were long established Scotland stars, and others who had become part of the folklore of Ibrox for their on-field exploits. That prince of goalkeepers Jerry Dawson was the last line of defence. In front of him was centre half Jimmy Simpson, captain of his club and country and father of Ronnie Simpson who was to earn a European Cup medal with Celtic thirty years on. George Brown was at left half, Alex Venters and Bob McPhail were the inside forwards and Jimmy Smith was the burly centre forward. Thornton, still a sixteen year old, was played at outside right, a position he had never played in before.

'But that kind of fact didn't trouble the Old Man,' he smiles. 'He thought that I was ready for the first team and that was that. I was going in and if outside right was the place he felt I should play then that was that. He believed a player should be able to play anywhere he was asked to play within reason. I was a forward and so I would play in the forward line and that was good enough. Actually I wasn't going to complain anyway. Why should I?

'This was still several months before I could sign professional forms at seventeen. I was plucked from the enclosure at Firhill and told I was playing. It was a League game against Partick Thistle and we won and I stayed in the team for the next six or seven games before I was dropped.

'I'll never forget that either. We had gathered at St Enoch's Hotel, which was where the team met in those days, and we were to travel down to Dumfries to play Queen of the South in a Scottish Cup game. Naturally I presumed that I would be going – and that I would be playing.

'Instead Mr Struth told me that I was playing in the reserves. They had an important game at Ibrox he explained, against Celtic Reserves and I was to play in that match. I was disappointed but I didn't say too much – I just went along to Ibrox and played for the second team. Funnily enough the first team lost 1–0 at Palmerston and were knocked out of the Cup so I missed a defeat. That was some consolation for me that night!'

Soon Thornton, who signed as a full professional in March 1937, took over as centre forward, the position he was to make his own. The man in possession was Jimmy Smith and Thornton recalls a funny story about the first time he was handed Smith's No 9 jersey.

'I was being pushed for the first team at this stage,' he says, 'by Davie Meiklejohn who had been club captain but was now

16

Striker Bobby Williamson, out for most of last year with a broken leg,
but earlier tipped to become another Willie Thornton

playing out his last year with Rangers in the reserves. Meek liked me and he kept pushing my claims for a place in the first team. Well, this day I was named in the pool of players to travel to Brockville to play against Falkirk. Now, up to this time, my first team appearances had been strictly limited to the outside right position and heading for the game at Falkirk I presumed, quite naturally, that the same thing would happen. So did big Smithy!

'When we got off the team bus we had to walk down a narrow road to the players entrance at Brockville – it's much the same today as it was then. On the way down Jimmy was talking away to me, taking me under his wing so to speak, and telling me that the left back was a bit of a hard man and I would have to be careful. But, he stressed, he would be there and some of the other older players and they would all look out for me. Imagine the surprise, then, in the dressing room when I was told I was to be centre forward and Jimmy was left out. It was a Scottish Cup game and it was an important match but I was in and he was dropped. . . .

'And the story didn't end there. Jimmy was from the village of Slamannan not too far away from Falkirk and a lot of his relatives had turned out for the match. Aunties and uncles and cousins and the rest and they had come to Brockville to see Jimmy play and there they were outside and Jimmy had to explain to them that he wasn't going to be playing. So he told them that when there were two players bidding for the same position, the manager tossed a coin to decide which one played in the team – and this time he had lost the toss!

'I suppose Jimmy was just trying to save a little bit of face in front of his family but he was overheard saying this.

'Someone who was a shareholder in Rangers overheard this explanation, thought that it was a terrible way to run a football team and raised the matter at the next annual meeting. Well, of course, he was told in no uncertain terms by Mr Struth that this was NOT the way that teams were picked. And that it would NEVER be the way that Rangers teams were picked. There was quite a fuss at the time and all caused because I had been given my first chance in the first team at centre forward.

'That trouble apart, I always look back on that game fondly. I played against Bob Shankly, who was later to manage Third Lanark, Falkirk, Dundee and Hibs, and scored the winning goal. I was convinced then that I would be able to win a Scottish Cup medal with Rangers that year, 1938. And when it came to the draw for the semi-finals I was even more certain that I would get that medal. One semi-final paired East Fife with St

Bernard's while we were drawn to meet Kilmarnock. All of us thought it would be a formality and that it would then be a walkover in the final against one of the lesser teams.

'It didn't turn out that way at all. Instead, we lost 4–3 to Kilmarnock and in the end little East Fife went on to win the Cup. They remain the only Second Division side ever to win the Scottish Cup. I had to wait until after the War, 1948 in fact, to win my first Scottish Cup medal, after a replay with Morton.'

It was after the War that Thornton experienced the finest days of his career. Championship medals, Scottish Cup medals, League Cup medals and Scottish international caps all showered in on the centre forward whose deadly partnership with right winger Willie Waddell was often overshadowed by the Iron Curtain defence which was always reckoned to be the cornerstone of the Ibrox successes in those days.

With George Young and Jock Shaw, Ian McColl, Willie Woodburn and Sammy Cox around, it's easy to see how the legends surrounding that great defence grew over the years.

But Thornton points out: 'You have to remember that we didn't have too bad a forward line then either. I know that people talk about the Iron Curtain team. And for attacking play they will talk about the Famous Five at Easter Road when Hibs had a forward line of Gordon Smith, Bobby Johnstone, Lawrie Reilly, Eddie Turnbull and Willie Ormond. That was a marvellous forward line but I don't think we were too bad. We had Willie Waddell and myself and we had Torry Gillick, Jimmy Duncanson, Eddie Rutherford. . . .

'OK, the defence was superb but don't run away with the idea that we were only there to make up the numbers. That was far from the truth. We had our moments . . . maybe we weren't praised in the same way as our defence or the Hibs front line but we could play a little bit.'

But while Thornton goes out of his way to praise the entire forward line and there are those who will single out Torry Gillick and others who will have their favourites, the Waddell-Thornton partnership was special.

It was feared and respected in Scotland and throughout the whole of Britain. The surging right-wing dashes by Waddell, the crosses and the headers of Thornton, using the skills he had taught himself in the miners' rows of his native village.

He recalls: 'These were great days – the best of my career. I have never seen anyone who could cross a ball on the run the way that Deedle (Willie Waddell) did. It's a lost art nowadays. Willie Johnston could do it but I don't think there's anyone left in the game who can do it now.

'Deedle could do it perfectly. He would be racing down that right wing, go past the full back and then sling the ball into the middle – and all at full speed. No hesitation. No let up. No pausing to get the ball under better control. He didn't need to do that. He could just get the ball across into the goalmouth and what crosses they were for a centre forward. It was tremendous playing with him out there on the wing. Torry Gillick used to say to wee Jimmy Caskie that he used to skin his nose on the ground going for his crosses – it was never that way with Deedle. They were struck perfectly.'

Thornton, of course, had a natural heading ability which he had worked on as a youngster back in Winchburgh. He explains: 'We used to play "heidies" in the pit row. You could be against one of your pals and you would be playing with the gable end of the buildings on, say, your right hand side to start with. Then when one of you had scored six goals you turned round and played with the wall on the other side. So we used to hit the ball against that gable end and developed our heading from each side. We used to do that for hour after hour and eventually it all paid off for me.

'I did have the ability to jump and time the jump and that came naturally but I still worked on heading. I believe to this day that you should work on players' strengths and improve them when you are training or coaching and Willie Waddell believed in that too when he was a manager.

'I mean there was no point in asking Jim Baxter to become a sprinter or to develop his right foot. These parts of his game were always going to be weak. But his left foot was extra special and so letting him work away on his passing with that foot improved on what was there naturally.

'I did that with Alan Gilzean when he was a young player at Dundee.

'Gilly wasn't the fastest player around then, or later on. And when he first turned up at Dens one or two people wondered if he would make the grade. But he had this natural ability in the air and I worked with him on that. I had him practising for hours and at the end of the day it paid off. He was an outstanding player with Dundee and went on to become a hero with Spurs and with Scotland. It was a case of concentrating on his good points instead of wasting time trying to improve something in his game which would, possibly, never be right.

'I mean, why try to teach Jim Baxter to tackle like Sammy Cox? That wouldn't have made any sense. Baxter was a fabulous player.

'I've always tried to follow that philosophy since Torry Gillick told me a story about Dixie Dean at Everton. Torry played at Goodison with Dixie, who was probably the most famous centre forward of all time in English football, and he told me something of the background to his heading power. Apparently at one stage of his life Dixie had been in a car crash and in the accident his legs were weakened and so he concentrated 100 per cent on building up his aerial power. That was everything for him and it paid off. That lesson stayed with me all through my time in football.'

Constant comparisons are made between Thornton's days and the troubled times we have now; comparisons between the on-field greats and the off-field problems. . . .

He says: 'It's hard to make comparisons between teams. But

Outside right Willie Henderson, another member of that famous sixties team Thornton enthuses over

Willie Thornton in his assistant manager role at a press conference
with former Rangers player Doug Baillie in the background

if I was pushed into it then I would think that the Iron Curtain
team was a better all round team than the famous side Rangers
had in the sixties. But that sixties side was more attractive. Look
at the forward line Willie Henderson, Ian McMillan, Jimmy
Millar, Ralph Brand and Davy Wilson. And behind them, Jim
Baxter. But maybe all round we were more efficient. It's hard
to say. Both teams lifted all the honours available. Both teams
had great individual stars. Let's just say they were two of the
greatest teams in the long history of Rangers Football Club!'

As for the troubles Thornton notes: 'I played in Hampden
Cup finals in front of crowds of over 130,000 and there was no
trouble. It's hard to understand the problems now but I think
the changing communities haven't helped. When I was at
Partick Thistle as manager the support was local – Maryhill
people who followed the team week after week. Now you go
back and Maryhill has disappeared and the families have been
scattered to the suburbs.

'That's a recent development – but the same thing is
happening to the Rangers supporters. Goven has changed,
Paisley Road has been knocked down in huge areas and so the
support has moved away. In that way the family atmosphere
where father took their sons along to the local ground has
disappeared to a large extent. So youngsters go to games on
their own, often travelling fair distances across the country or
across cities and they are unsupervised and so you get trouble.

22

People have to remember that this is a social evil. It's not football's fault that hooligans have attached themselves to some clubs. They are the type of people who would cause bother no matter where they were.

'It's just unhappy that football is a focal point for so many of them. It hurts when you see what is happening to the game.

'In my playing days we didn't have European competition but we did play friendlies. We would play Benfica or Racing Club of Paris or we would play in England and there was no trouble. In particular we had a very close relationship with Arsenal over the years and I recall Rangers going south to Highbury to open their floodlights. It was back in 1951 or 1952 and they had a wonderful team. Joe Mercer was still playing, Ray Daniel was at centre half against me, Red Forbes was the other wing half and Jimmy Logie was their star inside right. We were winning 1–0 with two minutes to play and they beat us 2–1. But what a great game, what a great occasion and it was always the same when we met Arsenal. These were show

One winger who reminded Thornton of his old playing partner Willie Waddell was ex-Ibrox star Willie Johnston who could cross a ball on the run the way Waddell did

games and people were there to see a great game of football – not to cause trouble on the terracings.'

Thornton's playing career ended in 1954 when he was thirty-four and he took over as Dundee manager. 'I went straight from playing with Rangers to being manager at Dundee and looking back now it's amazing how naive I was,' he smiles.

'Being with Rangers and under Bill Struth I believed that the club was run solely by the manager. At Ibrox you would see directors occasionally. They might come into the dressing rooms and say a few words before a game but when they had gone out the Old Man would tell you to forget every word they had spoken.

'So I went into my first managerial job not realizing the power that directors could have. Even at Dens Park the one man I knew was George Anderson who was managing director there. He offered me the job I accepted and I didn't meet anyone else until I took over the job.

'That was the way football was run in those days!'

Thornton had happy times with Dundee, and went on to become manager of Partick Thistle, another job he enjoyed hugely. But, he admits now, his heart always remained at Ibrox.

In 1968 when Davie White was manager, Thornton was invited back to take over as assistant manager and until last year he retained that position during some turbulent times at the famous Ibrox Stadium. Most of the time he was content to remain in the background, a link with the great days of Struth and with the days of such success both before and after the War. He had been signed by the great man, played with his successor Scot Symon and then served under four more Rangers managers as their right-hand man – Davie White, his old comrade-in-arms Willie Waddell, Jock Wallace and John Greig.

He has officially retired now and was honoured by the Rangers Supporters' Association, but he still goes to Ibrox most mornings to 'keep in touch with things'.

He maintains: 'Even if I was away from the club I'd still be going to see them every week. I had good times as a manager at Dens Park and Firhill but Rangers is in my blood. Bill Struth made all of us Rangers minded, he made us think about the club at all times and that never leaves you.

'I was away for fourteen years – but deep down I never really left. It was the happiest day of my life when I was asked to go back there. And even now, almost fifty years on, it seems like yesterday that Bill Struth offered me one pound a week to play for Rangers and told me to go to Clydebank and see that ship that was being built. . . .'

HAVE BOOTS~WILL TRAVEL!
by Ally McCoist

If anyone had told me while I was still playing with Sunderland
that I'd travel the equivalent of almost twice round the world
in a single football season then I would probably have laughed
out loud.

But when you play for a team like Rangers that can happen
to you quite easily because you are with a club that the whole
world wants to see in action.

Striker Ally McCoist is bundled off this ball by Dundee United's
international defender Richard Gough

That is the difference between playing with a reasonably well known top League club in Scotland or England and playing with a really famous team. Wherever football is played people know about Rangers and Celtic from Scotland just as they know about Arsenal, Liverpool and Manchester United from England.

OK, I accept that Aberdeen and Dundee United have made their mark in Europe over the past few seasons but the Old Firm's appeal stretches all the way out to Australia and New Zealand and then back across the United States and Canada. I should know because that was exactly the trip we undertook

Here is McCoist, the Skol Cup's top scorer, in full flight!

in the 1984 close season. And everywhere we went we found Rangers supporters waiting to welcome us.

It's only when you go on a long trip such as that one that you realize the power of the club's appeal. Exiled Scots see the team as a symbol of home, and the sides you are asked to play against see you as one of the most famous teams in the world. Which guarantees that they'll raise their game and that no trip can ever be a holiday jaunt when you are a Rangers player!

Whenever you walk through the imposing front doors of Ibrox and into the marble hall you know that the club is special. But if you ever had any doubts just one lengthy tour with the team would demonstrate the bond which exists between the club and the supporters. No matter how far they are from home! It is honestly quite incredible.

Anyhow, the summer of 1984 saw me start off on a soccer season which was to be my most travelled ever. First of all, there we were in Australia playing a series of games against national selects – and hard games they were too – and then it was on to New Zealand for more matches to round off the first leg of that round-the-world trip. Then we crossed the Pacific and made our way to Minneapolis for one game there in the States and finished up with two matches in Toronto.

It was a fabulous trip and an important one for all of us despite the bad luck which seemed to dog the players – or, at least, those unlucky enough to share a room with me. But I'll get to that later. First, let's get on with the travel talk.

That trip came at the end of the previous season. There was a short breather then we took off because the manager Jock Wallace believed that a long tour at that time would help us get a real team understanding going and also help build morale. It was a formula which had worked for him before and I think that's why he repeated it.

But it wasn't all he did in the close season. For just before the season kicked off we were off on our travels again, to play pre-season warm-up games in Switzerland and West Germany. These were designed to get rid of any rustiness, to help have us match fit and to prepare us for playing in Europe.

That was to be one of our major targets of the season, a long run in the UEFA Cup, after our victory in the League Cup had won a place for us. Our first game was a let down – difficult when it came to getting a result but a disappointment for the fans who wanted to see some of the glamour teams from the Continent arrive at Ibrox. The passports were left at home for that first round game against Bohemians in Dublin.

Then for the second round we were drawn against Inter Milan

and all their stars. So Italy could be added to the half dozen countries I'd already been to and the season hadn't reached the halfway stage yet.

Unhappily we lost in that match and out we went – but the travelling didn't stop. In the spring the Boss decided that we should go abroad again, this time to the Middle East where we played two games against the Iraq national team in Baghdad and another match against Kuwait in Jordan.

So there I was – in less than a year I'd been almost twice around the world in distance terms and I'd played football in NINE different countries. Have boots, will travel is certainly the case when you join up at Ibrox.

But, as I said earlier, these trips are not jaunts. Obviously the European games are competitive in the very real sense of the word, but the other games can be just as difficult.

The games we had in Australia were as physical as you get anywhere in the world. We had heard the game was tough over there – and believe me it was. They don't take many prisoners. . . .

I think it's because there are a few lads out there who emigrated from Britain, lads from Scotland and England who know that you have arrived there with a fair reputation and want to prove that they can play as well as you can. So they get wired in. We had been warned so it wasn't unexpected – but it was still tough. We played five games there against their national select sides. Their 'A' team beat us 3–2 in one game but we were able to beat their 'B' side three times and draw with them once before we moved on to New Zealand.

But it was off the field that bad luck struck worst of all. My room-mate Bobby Williamson tried to jump a small fence at our hotel, stumbled, fell badly and ended up with a broken leg in an Australian hospital. And it virtually wiped him out for the whole of last season. It was only towards the end that he had recovered enough to start pushing his way towards the first team again. That was a bad blow for Bobby and for the team. Then Colin McAdam moved in to room with me and he broke his leg in a game!

I was the jinx of the trip, I think, because the bad luck didn't end there. Sandy Clark stepped into the breach next and he ended up needing half a dozen stitches in a head injury. Now on trips, I have Cammy Fraser as my 'roomie' and so far he has managed to avoid the bad luck which struck on that tour. I'm keeping my fingers crossed things stay that way!

The most important game of the tour was probably the one in Toronto when we played Stuttgart who had finished the season as champions of West Germany. Now I happen to think that the Bundesliga is one of the top leagues in Europe so coming up against them and drawing 1–1 was quite an achievement for us. They were there with almost their full strength team, just a couple of players were missing so it was a real test for us at the end of the trip.

Ally McCoist finds out how close the marking is in the Premier League as he has to combat the attentions of Celtic's Murdo MacLeod

That is the kind of game I enjoy most of all because you are tested fully and can increase your knowledge of the game. There are obviously different approaches in different countries and in West Germany you tend to find that the defenders go man for man against the opposing attackers with a 'sweeper' playing free behind them. I don't mind that. There is fairly close marking to combat in the Premier League which prepares you for that type of opposition. And with the 'sweeper' lying that little bit further back you can find space if you get clear of the player who is marking you. It's a battle of wits – and of strength – but I enjoy it.

In a sense that game helped prepare me for the match against Inter Milan – though nothing could properly prepare you for

McCoist's fellow striker Bobby Williamson whose broken leg marred the close-season trip Down Under

playing in the San Siro Stadium for the first time. I don't think I've ever played in that kind of atmosphere before. It is awesome. About an hour before the kick-off we went out to take a look at the ground and there were maybe forty thousand fans already there in the stadium, and the feeling was hostile. All that time before the kick-off they were jeering and spitting at us. Some of the lads had played in these conditions before but for most of us it was new and it was pretty frightening.

That was a difficult game for me. I was asked to play up front more or less on my own and battle it out with the Italian defence. The idea was for me to get the ball, hold it and allow support to come up from the midfield. I might have scored, too. In fact, I should have scored when it was only 1–0 for them. But I hurried my shot and the chance was missed. It was the kind of opening that I should be able to put away every time but in the circumstances I snatched at the ball, the chance disappeared and you know the rest of the story. Inter went on to score two late goals in the San Siro and though we hit back at Ibrox we went out by a single goal.

Yes, my goal could have made all the difference to the result. I worried over that at the time but I don't worry any more. I don't think that it would be professional to sit and brood over one missed chance, no matter how much it might have cost the team. If I did then I could end up worrying every time the ball came to me. I can't afford that – I have to get on with the job. I have to try to keep scoring goals, try to keep playing at my best. Sitting moping won't help me do that . . . even though it did haunt me for a week or two after the UEFA Cup tie.

It would have been nice to go on into the next round. I know that the Boss desperately wants to have a good long run in Europe. I think he would like to see the team do well there in a testing arena which is different from the one at home. He has been over the course before when the team won the European Cup Winners' Cup. That must have been tremendous for everyone connected with Rangers and I think he would like to see it repeated. So would we all. Of course, there is always a spin-off at home when you do well in Europe. It increases the team's confidence and the more players are away together the better the understanding is between us all. That's why we go on tour and Europe would be an even bigger help as regards that.

I know that my own form fluctuated last season, from doing quite well in the League Cup, or the Skol Cup as it is now known, to fading a bit during the middle part of the season. Then coming away strongly at the end.

The finishing run of the season was good for me. The last game against Hibs was the only one of the final dozen where I didn't manage to score. In that spell I grabbed thirteen goals in eleven games and I finished up the team's top scorer for the season. But I want to do better next season and keep my form all the way through the year. If I can work at that then maybe I can help the team challenge for the Premier League title – which is what we all want to win at Ibrox. Last season, after the disappointment of our New Year's Day defeat from Celtic we slumped badly. We can't afford to let that happen again and I'm sure all of us know that.

Funnily enough the Skol Cup has been a tournament which has been good to me. Last year I was the top scorer in the whole competition and that won me a summer holiday in St Kitt's – another part of the world to add to my globe-trotting activities. And the year before I scored a hat-trick in the Old Firm final against Celtic. If I could transfer that form to the League then I'd be happy. Mind you all I really want is to start off the season where it finished for me. Honestly I didn't want the season to come to an end despite the fact that we had lost out in the League and the Scottish Cup. The way I was playing, the way the goals were coming and the way my confidence had

McCoist's fellow striker Iain Ferguson turns away after scoring against Hibs

returned, I would quite happily have played on right through the summer.

Of course our summer preparation had to be altered following the Brussels tragedy at the European Cup final. We were heading back to West Germany, but the club pulled out of the games in case there could be trouble. So we had to wait for Europe before looking out the passports again.

The League and Europe will always be our major targets. The first one proves that you are the best team at home. Winning the Skol Cup or the Scottish Cup is fine, but winning the League is always the best thing that can happen to any side. That is the true test, when you have to prove yourselves over thirty-six games and unfortunately we failed to do that last year. So now we want to do it even more and I believe that we can. At the same time, we would dearly love a long run in the UEFA Cup. If we can combine the two dreams then we can say we have had a successful season . . . .

But if we fail then we know that the supporters will be demanding success in the two Cup competitions instead. When you are with Rangers you are not allowed to relax. The support wants success and we all know that we have to provide it for them.

Another member of last season's Ibrox strike force, Dave Mitchell in a race for this ball with Hibs centre half Gordon Rae. Mitchell has now returned to Australia

MOSCOW DYNAMO COME BACK TO IBROX

The rivalry between Rangers and the famous Russian team Moscow Dynamo stretches back four decades. Back to that famous tour made by the Russians just after the war when ninety thousand people crammed into Ibrox to see the first foreign team to play in Britain since the late 1930s.

And what a team that was. There are still those around who talk with reverence of that side and of the day they came to Ibrox at the end of their British tour. By then they had played three games, drawing 3–3 with Chelsea at Stamford Bridge, beating Cardiff City 10–1 and following that up with a victory over Arsenal, who fielded Stanley Matthews as a guest player, by 4–3.

Weeks before the game Ibrox had been sold out. Queues snaked around the Glasgow streets as the tickets went on sale in the main agency in the centre of the city. Traffic was stopped as the fans snapped up the tickets for the biggest game to be staged in the city since before the war.

The fans had been starved of soccer – especially the international class soccer which the crack Russians had been providing on their British tour. Here they were, just six months after the end of the war, with Glasgow waiting to greet them and, eventually, to enshrine them in football folklore.

Of all their players the most famous was to be their goalkeeper Tiger Khomich. A generation of schoolboys volunteered to play in goal in thousands of street games just so long as they could try to emulate Khomich.

Their centre forward was Konstantin Beskov, later to become their manager and manager of the international team. He was in charge when Rangers played them in Barcelona in the final of the European Cup Winners' Cup in 1972. That, despite the off field troubles with the fans and the Spanish police, strengthened the ties which had been forged back in 1945. Which was why Jock Wallace jumped at the chance of another game against the Russians when a British tour was scheduled during the winter shut-down which affects most of Eastern Europe.

Enthused Wallace: 'This is the kind of game we need as a team – one to provide the players with European experience. And it's a way of celebrating the past. This club has great traditions and we want to uphold them.'

So much is tradition valued at Ibrox that Wallace arranged for many of the players who had faced Dynamo before to be at the game and to take their bows before the new faces kicked off. How well he succeeded in arranging the soccer pageant which brought together four Rangers managers as well as the players who had faced the Russians in 1945 and then in Barcelona in 1972.

The managers who appeared on the pitch were Scot Symon, making a return to Ibrox for the first time as a spectator since being sacked by the club eighteen years earlier; Willie Waddell who, like Symon, had played in 1945, then managed Rangers when they won their only European trophy against the Russians in Barcelona; John Greig who had been skipper of the European

The line-up of past heroes who played against Moscow Dynamo down through the years: at the back Peter McCloy and John Greig; second back row, Colin Stein, Willie Johnston, Derek Johnstone, Alex MacDonald, Alex Miller, Tommy McLean and Jock Wallace; next row, Sandy Jardine, Jimmy Duncanson, Willie Waddell, Willie Mathieson; next row, Scot Symon, Jimmy Smith, Billy Williamson, Jock Shaw; front row, George Young, Davie Gray and Charlie Johnstone

Cup Winners' Cup winning team and then later managed the club for six years; and the present boss Jock Wallace, right-hand man to Waddell in Barcelona and now back at the helm after his exile in Leicester.

Nine of the greats who met up with Dynamo in 1945 were led onto the pitch by the man who captained them on that famous afternoon – Jock 'Tiger' Shaw. Following Shaw were Davie Gray, George Young, Scot Symon, Willie Waddell, Jimmy Smith, Billy Williamson, Charlie Johnstone and Jimmy Duncanson who was used as a substitute.

And from the 1972 team came John Greig, goalkeeper Peter McCloy, in action again this time around, Sandy Jardine, Willie Mathieson, Derek Johnstone, Tommy McLean, Colin Stein, Alex MacDonald and Willie Johnston.

It was an impressive turn out and the twelve thousand supporters who turned out on a bitterly cold night wallowed happily in nostalgia.

Perhaps, on the night the game did not turn out as memorable as the previous games. No one will talk of this clash as people still talk of the 1945 meeting and of the historic Cup Winners' Cup final. But, then, the stories and legends still grow around these earlier clashes.

No one who was there in 1945 can forget Jock Shaw's embarrassment when the Russian captain presented him with a bouquet of flowers before the kick off. . . .

No one can forget, either, how the Russians were caught out playing with twelve men at one stage of the match. . . .

And no one can forget the fierce duels between Rangers' burly centre forward Jimmy Smith and the powerful Dynamo goalkeeper Tiger Khomich.

All of these incidents were relived after the game as the old players gathered. It was the late Torry Gillick who spotted that the Russians had an extra man on the field and he pointed it out to the referee, aided by little Charlie Johnstone. The Russians explained that it was all a mistake but Gillick had been quick enough to spot the ploy. Remember, this was well before substitutes were being used in our game and seeing changes being made during a match was a novelty. Not one that the fans then liked. And not one that the players particularly approved of either!

So when one Russian was supposed to leave the field he stayed on to link up with his replacement – the always razor sharp Gillick was the man who stepped in to put an end to that little bit of nonsense!

Jimmy Smith was injured in one of his clashes with Khomich,

but it was in that incident that he scored the opening goal for Rangers at a time when they trailed 2–0 just before half time.

Recalls Smith: 'They were a very strong team physically but that was never a thing to upset me. I was six feet and fourteen stones so I could handle myself OK in that type of game.

'Khomich used to come out of his goal for a ball with his feet high and aiming for any forward who might be challenging him. The manager, Bill Struth, asked how I would cope with this

Below left: Goalkeeper Peter McCloy who has now played against Moscow Dynamo in the Cup Winners' Cup final in Barcelona and again at Ibrox on the nostalgic return

Below right: Derek Johnstone was the man Dynamo feared – but it was skipper Craig Paterson who grabbed the only goal of the game to give Rangers their Ibrox victory

Rangers midfield man Robert Russell, in action here against Alan McInally of Celtic, was the man who set up the Rangers goal against the Russians with a perfectly placed free kick

problem. I had decided by this time to get in first. That's how I got the goal – and it's also how I was injured and had to leave the field before the end of the match. But the goal kept us alive. . . .'

It did indeed. The Russians had scored twice, through Kartsev after just three minutes and then again in twenty-five minutes. Between these goals Willie Waddell missed a penalty kick for the Scots and so Smith's goal coming before the interval was vital.

In the second half Billy Williamson was fouled in the penalty box, this time George Young took the kick and equalised and that was how the game ended. Afterwards the Russians praised the Rangers team. A spokesman said: 'They were the fittest team we played in the whole of our tour of Britain. And they gave us our most difficult game. We did not expect their standard to be so high.'

The men who kept it high those forty years ago were Jerry Dawson; Davie Gray, Jock Shaw; Charlie Watkins, George Young, Scot Symon; Willie Waddell, Torry Gillick, Jimmy Smith, Billy Williamson and Charlie Johnstone.

There was one more game between the teams before the epic encounter in Spain. Two years earlier they played in a friendly at Ibrox, still cementing the good relations which existed between the two great clubs. Rangers won 1–0 with a header from Derek Johnstone giving Rangers their victory.

But it's Barcelona which is the main memory for the present fans. That night in Spain when Rangers became only the second team in Scottish football history to win a European trophy. The team then was: Peter McCloy; Sandy Jardine, Willie Mathieson; John Greig, Derek Johnstone, Dave Smith; Tommy McLean, Alfie Conn, Colin Stein, Alex MacDonald and Willie Johnston.

It was a night which will live on forever in the memories of the thousands of fans who had made the trek across Europe to the Camp Nou Stadium in Barcelona and of the millions who watched at home. Rangers had marched through Europe in magnificent fashion that year. In the first round they had defeated the French team Rennes, then Sporting Lisbon fell to them in Portugal. In the quarter-finals their victims were Torino of Italy and in the last four they defeated Bayern Munich, then at the height of their powers. The West Germans had a clutch of current international players – goalkeeper Sepp Maier, defenders George Schwarzenbeck, Franz Beckenbauer and Paul Breitner, midfield men Werner Roth and Uli Hoeness and up front the incomparable goal-scoring machine, Gerd Muller.

Rangers had beaten them all to reach the final of the tournament for the third time. On their previous appearances they had lost to Fiorentina in a two-legged affair, then to Bayern after extra time in Nuremberg. Now they wanted to win it and they believed they could do it.

Inside forty-eight amazing minutes everyone in Europe believed they would do it too. For, by then, Rangers were three goals ahead. That scoring spree had started in just twenty-four minutes when their sweeper Dave Smith set up a chance for striker Colin Stein who smashed a marvellous shot past Pilgui in the Dynamo goal.

A few minutes before half time Willie Johnston scored a second and then he repeated that in forty-eight minutes as the huge Rangers support went wild on the terracings.

It seemed all over but, in the end, on that night of so many sensations, Rangers were hanging on desperately to stop the game going into extra time. How the Russians fought back. They scored after an hour and they scored another three minutes from the end of the game. Somehow Rangers survived and a bearded John Greig lifted the trophy the club had been dreaming of since European competitions started some sixteen years earlier.

So it was on to the present day, to February 1985 to be precise and the fourth meeting between the two clubs. Dynamo arrived at Ibrox with a mixed reputation. They had the historical background, of course, as one of the great Russian club sides. Champions of that huge country on eleven occasions, Cup winners on another six occasions and currently the Cup holders. But, in spite of winning the Cup in the previous season they had suffered badly in the League championship. Only a point saved them from the humiliation of relegation to the Second Division. They picked up only twenty-six points from their thirty-four League matches scoring thirty-four goals and losing forty-three. Hardly an inspiring record.

Yet they did win the Cup and when they arrived at Ibrox they had already reached the quarter-finals of the Cup Winners' Cup. They were to go still further in that tournament and their veteran striker Valeri Gazzayev who lined up against Rangers was their danger man.

Dynamo wanted games in Britain to avoid losing impetus for their Cup Winners' Cup bid during their own country's winter break. Rangers were an obvious choice. The Russians knew of their tremendous fight back against Inter Milan. They knew of their long European history and they knew, too, of the bond of friendship between the sides. It was the right place for them to kick off their short British visit. Unfortunately they found it difficult to demonstrate the form which had inspired them in their domestic Cup and in the European tournament. But for the Rangers players it was a chance to taste top class European opposition again. That was why Jock Wallace was wanting to play Dynamo in the first place.

The game was settled just short of the hour mark when the free kicks which had been so useful to Rangers throughout the season paid off yet again. This time Robert Russell took the kick and while Dynamo concentrated all their attentions on Derek Johnstone, newly returned from Chelsea, Craig Paterson roared into the penalty area to flight a header out of the reach of the Russian keeper Prudnikkov. That was enough to give Rangers victory and to push them still further ahead of Dynamo in the results of the games which have taken place between the two clubs. The Russians have still to gain their first win after four games against the Scots. They have now lost twice at Ibrox and once in Spain, all by one goal. Their closest to success was that 2–2 draw in 1945.

And that game will still be remembered long after the latest match in the series. But watching the old heroes parade across Ibrox once more was worth the visit. Nostalgia rules, OK!

Action man Ted McMinn one of the 'new faces' who played against Moscow Dynamo on that night of nostalgia at Ibrox

SO CLOSE TO GLORY AGAINST INTER MILAN

Inter Milan were a team determined to regain former glories when Rangers were drawn against them in the second round of the UEFA Cup.

The glorious days when they had dominated European football under the ruthless regime of Helenio Herrera, the high priest of 'cattanaccio', that so-Italian tactical plan based on deep defence, had long gone. One of the games which ended their dominance was in Lisbon in 1967 when Celtic became the first British club to win the European Cup. It was recognized as the death-knell for Herrera's tactics and Inter had suffered since.

Under Herrera in the sixties they had won the European Cup twice in succession and added the world club championship to it each time. Following his reign they had not managed a single European trophy win. Their best effort was when they were beaten finalists in 1972. They wanted more than that and in the summer of 1984 they made massive moves to strengthen their team for an assault on the Italian championship and another attempt to force their way back into Europe's elite by winning the UEFA Cup.

Their directors authorized the signing of Liam Brady from Sampdoria and Karl Heinz Rummenigge from Bayern Munich at a cost of three and a half million pounds. In addition to that they lured Ilario Castagnen from bitter local rivals AC Milan to take over as the Inter coach. That move from bossing one of the Milan clubs to bossing the other shocked the whole of Italy and left the bustling city of Milan even more deeply divided on the football front.

But Inter and their fans didn't care about the divisions being caused. All they wanted was to upstage their city rivals who had bought the English pair of Mark Hateley and Butch Wilkins and brought back Nils Liedholm from Roma to be their coach.

An Italian contact of mine explained to me: 'Neither of the two teams can afford to have the other looking as if they will push ahead whether that is on or off the field. If one buys big new names then the other MUST follow. That is the way of life in the city and nothing will change it.'

Then he added significantly: 'Inter are becoming more and more determined to win a European trophy. They will do everything in their power to make sure that they beat Rangers. To go out so early would be a disaster which they could not handle.'

For Rangers, too, an early exit would be disastrous; though, while manager Jock Wallace had spent money in the close season, it could in no way match the extravagances of Inter. Wallace's signings of Cammy Fraser and Iain Ferguson from Dundee were big by Scottish standards – four hundred thousand pounds for the two men he wanted – but a mere fraction of what Inter had spent on their two foreign players.

As always Jock Wallace went to the San Siro in Milan to see his opponents in action. He returned impressed, but not overawed. 'You only have to look at the team list before the game to know that you will be watching quality players,' he pointed out on his return. 'If you have people like Collovatti, Altobelli, Brady and Rummenigge available then you are going

Australian striker Davie Mitchell, always a menace to the Inter defence, is sent tumbling by a hefty challenge from Collovatti in the second-leg game at Ibrox

The sight which thrilled the thirty thousand Ibrox fans – Iain Ferguson
who scored twice, in full cry in the UEFA Cup second-leg clash.
Here he leaves Baresi stranded as he races for goal

to be a handy outfit. But there were one or two things I noticed
which we will be working on before playing the first leg over
there.'

Going to the San Siro brought its own worries. That fearsome
stadium which is shared by the two Milan teams, had been a
graveyard for every Scottish team to play there in European
competition. Rangers themselves lost there to Inter in the European Cup quarter-final in 1965. They went down 3–1 before
going out on aggregate by 3–2. Hearts lost 4–0 to Inter and
Dundee crashed 5–1 to AC Milan. Then Celtic notched a hat-
trick of failures. They drew twice in the San Siro against AC
and then Inter – but lost both games at Celtic Park. And
between these two, Rangers' Old Firm rivals lost to Feyenoord
in the final of the European Cup in 1970.

There was not much to be gained by studying the record
books. Instead Wallace knew that he must impress on his new
players that they had the ability to close down Inter in the first-
leg game. He wanted to frustrate them and to get the Italian
fans to turn against their own team. He knew that Inter had
not started the season the way their fans had demanded. And
he knew that Hateley had become the hero of Milan while the
blond German star Rummenigge had still to score a League

goal after costing a huge two million pounds transfer fee and promising the Milan support that he would score fifteen League goals for his new club.

Wallace learned all of that – noted that Rummenigge seemed unhappy in his new surroundings; saw that Brady was having problems in fitting into the Inter set up; recognized that the fans were far from happy with a team which did not have the look of potential champions. It was all important information for his dossier. . . .

And little Brady, the man Arsenal have tried to take back to Highbury so many times, confirmed the Ibrox manager's views. On the eve of the game against Rangers, and just after a disappointing 1–0 win over unfancied and unrated Como, the Eire international midfield man admitted: 'There are problems in the team. I know that I did not play well against Como and that's something that I have been discussing with the team coach. We must play better if we are to get a convincing win over Rangers.'

Rummenigge seemed more confident despite his personal scoring problems but he insisted: 'I have warned the other players here that we cannot expect to have things easy against Rangers. I know how strong and how hard-running the Scottish

Midfield man Cammy Fraser shows all his shooting power as he sends this drive for the Italian goal. Unluckily for Fraser and Rangers he was off target – but Iain Ferguson and Davie Mitchell were not as the Italians reeled to defeat!

teams can be. It's only eighteen months since I suffered a defeat with Bayern against Aberdeen in the Cup Winners' Cup.

'But all of the players know how important this game is for Inter. Last season the team won nothing and now they have spent big money and they want a return on their investments. All of us are aware of that and it is essential if we are to make Inter great again that we stay in Europe and to do that we must beat Rangers here in the San Siro Stadium. If we can win by two goals here, then the tie will be over. The style we play away from home would not allow us to lose more than a single goal unless something went drastically wrong with our planning. We have never lost many goals away from home before and it will be no different this time. The job has to be done here in front of our own supporters.'

There was no need for Wallace to psyche up his own players. They knew that they were coming up against some of the best players on the Continent and that they would be playing the game in one of the world's most famous arenas. As Wallace remarked: 'This kind of game builds the players for you. They all know what we have to do and I believe that we can achieve our aim here in Milan. I want a scoring draw and that is not beyond us. Inter have good players but I didn't see anything from them that would make me rate them any higher than Aberdeen or Dundee United or Celtic. We are asked to beat them back home in Scotland and so now we are asked to beat Inter in Europe. There's no difference.'

The major difference, however, was the fearsome San Siro itself. None of the Rangers players had ever played there before. Even veteran keeper Peter McCloy, set to make his forty-first appearance for Rangers in Europe, had not experienced the hostile atmosphere.

Twice he had played in Turin, each time with successful conclusions, against Torino and then against Juventus. But even McCloy knew and recognized that there was something different about San Siro, especially when that concrete bowl was filled with the volatile Inter fans.

The night before the game, Wallace announced his team and made his intentions plain. It was to be defensive. It could be nothing else to face the furious assaults the Italians had threatened to launch against the Scots.

But it was to be sensible defence based in the midfield rather than the backs-to-the-wall defending in their own penalty area which had cost Rangers dearly in the past.

It was a modern approach. Wallace intended to flood the midfield thus cutting down on the service to the Italian front men. He insisted: 'We are not running scared . . . we are simply being sensible. If we can get a scoring draw here then we can go through. That is our aim, to get at least one goal and to frustrate and contain them as much as possible.'

And so the Ibrox boss decided on a side with five midfield men – Robert Russell, Robert Prytz, Ian Redford, Cammy Fraser and, drafted in there specially for his dour, defensive qualities, Ally Dawson, normally recognized as a full back.

As sixty-five thousand fans watched they saw the Rangers ideas take shape early in the game. Young Dave McPherson was used behind the two central defenders as a spare man, there to cut off any through balls sent into the danger area by Liam Brady. In front of him Craig Paterson and Northern Ireland international John McClelland joined forces to combat the twin menace of Italian international Sandro Altobelli and the West German ace Karl Heinz Rummenigge. It was a task McClelland

Jock Wallace always felt that aerial power would worry the Italian defence. Here he is proved right as Dave Mitchell soars above the Inter rearguard to direct a header towards a half-hidden Iain Ferguson and midfielder Ian Redford

had performed with distinction playing for his country against West Germany and Rummenigge had grudgingly admitted in the build up to the game: 'McClelland is an awkward opponent and I know this from our games against Northern Ireland in the European Championships. He will be important for Rangers.'

On the night, though, it was Rummenigge who was to have revenge for his country's poor results in Europe.

It was Rummenigge who avoided his marker in just seventeen minutes when he moved effortlessly down the right flank before crossing a magnificent ball to the far post. Altobelli, also free, rose to head the ball back into goal and there was Antonio Sabato to finish things off with the Rangers strategy in tatters.

Then Altobelli stepped in to set up a second goal in sixty-six minutes for veteran Franco Causion who had appeared as a substitute just a couple of minutes earlier.

Then the two front men combined to wreck finally Rangers' hopes of a long run in Europe. Altobelli was the goal maker, and Rummenigge was the man who burst through the Scots defence to head the third goal only three minutes from the end.

Before that Ally McCoist had lofted a try over the bar from close range when it seemed certain that he would score. That would have – and should have – given Wallace the away goal he wanted. Instead the chance was missed and the task ahead of Rangers looked hopeless. Not only did they have to contemplate that three goal deficit for their home game at Ibrox in two weeks time, but they had to try to wipe out the memory of the defeat before the Skol Cup final against Dundee United at Hampden on the following Sunday. It was not a happy group which jetted back from Italy. . . .

Yet Wallace remained stubbornly defiant in face of all the odds. 'We will win the next leg against Inter,' he snapped. 'Maybe we will go out of the tournament now but we won't be going out without having a real go at them.

'If we were going back to the San Siro next week then I would play the same way. It didn't go too far wrong. We were unlucky to lose that very late goal, and earlier we had had a couple of chances. One of them in particular should have been put away. If that had gone in then people wouldn't be as critical of the tactics as they are being now. There were times in the game when we played with a lot of composure and that pleased me. Now we have to keep that composure for the Skol Cup and for the next leg and add some bite to it. We have to get the ball up front quicker than we have been doing.'

By the time Inter did arrive in Glasgow some of Wallace's optimism had been justified. The Rangers support had been

Opposite: Goal-scorer Iain Ferguson holds aloft the Skol League Cup

Above: Winger Davie Cooper who became a World Cup regular for Scotland last season

Opposite above: Dave McPherson shows the style which won him Hampden's Man of the Match award as he curbs the menace of Dundee United and Scotland striker Paul Sturrock

Opposite below: Ally Dawson breaks up a Hibs attack and bursts clear to put Rangers on the offensive

Above: Ally McCoist wins this heading duel with Hibs defender Alan Brazil

Opposite above: Rangers' Under-21 international Dave McPherson in confident action against Hibs in a Premier League clash last season

Opposite below: Relieved looks from Rangers players Dave McPherson, Robert Prytz and Craig Paterson as Dave McKinnon steps in to end a Hibs attack

Above right: Derek Johnstone brings the ball under control against Aberdeen shortly after his return from Chelsea

Above left: Defender Dave McKinnon beats Hearts' young goal-getter John Robertson to this ball in the Ibrox draw between the two teams

Below: A drive from Rangers striker Ally McCoist beats the diving St Mirren keeper Campbell Money, hits the post and ends up in the net

Above: Rangers' strike force of Iain Ferguson and Ally McCoist fight it out here with the Aberdeen and Scotland pairing of Willie Miller and Alex McLeish

Below left: Ian Redford's delight is obvious as he punches the air following his goal against Dumbarton

Below right: Close season signing from Dundee, midfielder Cammy Fraser

lifted by their second successive Skol League Cup win . . . and what they wanted now was to see some form of revenge taken against the Italians who strutted confidently into Glasgow and pledged that they would not lose a single goal against the Scots.

One of their forwards who had played in Milan, Giancarlo Pasinato, was left out to allow an extra defender to be brought in. Ricardo Ferri was the man who stepped back to bolster Inter's defence. They brought only a handful of fans with them on their charter flight. Other charters had been cancelled because, like the players, the supporters were planning for the next round. That's how confident they were . . . and with every right to be so. Never once had Inter lost three goals in a European game and, in spite of Jock Wallace's confident approach, not even the staunchest Rangers fans expected them to do it at Ibrox for the first time.

But coach Castagnen did not want his players to fall into the trap of over-confidence. He had seen it happen before and he warned against it as the team settled into their Glasgow hotel.

'Three seasons ago Roma lost a three-goal lead when they had to go to East Germany,' he pointed out to anyone who would listen. 'Their players thought the game was won in Rome. It was not and we cannot think that this game is won until we are on the plane back to Milan. We must look at this game as if we are starting all over again. We must defend but also we must be ready to attack. I will look for Liam Brady to push forward to support our front players. It is in the midfield that we must control the game. The key to the tie is there.'

By this stage Jock Wallace had no time for such niceties. As Rangers prepared at Turnberry for the second-leg game the Ibrox boss resorted to earthier sentiments. He wanted a win to wipe out the memory of the failure in Milan and he wanted that accomplished by fierce and committed attacking football.

'We'll go for their jugular,' he snarled in the quiet confines of the Turnberry Hotel. 'Nobody in the world gives us a chance but I believe that we can win the game – and even win the tie itself. OK you'll think I'm nuts but we have to go out after them tonight and make them realize very early on that they will not be allowed to coast through this match.

'I accept that if we do go through then it will be the best result any team I've managed has achieved. But I want that result and I want this team to go out and earn the respect of the fans again. If they stay behind us then a win is ON!'

The single statistic which could bring Wallace and his players some cheer was the appalling away record of Inter. As they approached the Ibrox game their previous eight away ties in

Europe had brought them defeats. And it was back in 1981 when they played a poorly rated Turkish team that they could last boast of a victory outside the San Siro.

Their coach Castagnen, still worrying over his team's attitude warned his players: 'We must hold Rangers at the start when they will hurl themselves forward to please their support and unsettle us. But it is not only then that we must be careful. In the last round they scored two late goals and we know that they are fit and strong and capable of going full out for the whole ninety minutes. And even into extra time if that is necessary.'

When Australian centre forward Davie Mitchell sent Rangers into the lead after five minutes of that second leg the thirty thousand fans began to believe in Wallace's prediction.

And that explosive start to the game brought this Rangers team to within touching distance of the club's most historic win in their thirty years of European competition.

And it was done without the skills and guile of Davie Cooper who had failed a last minute fitness test. Wallace juggled his side around, pushing Irish defender John McClelland up front

This time Cammy Fraser loses out in a heading duel with Inter's Mandorlini as Rangers try for the goal to keep them in the tourney

First taste of the big time. Stuart Munro, Rangers' second-half substitute, get's in a cross despite the challenge from an Italian defender

in a bid to hustle the Italian defence – and it was that move
which helped lead to the first goal.

McClelland headed a ball down for Cammy Fraser whose
shot was pushed out by the Inter goalkeeper. There was Mitchell
pouncing swiftly ahead of his markers to head the ball into the
net with keeper Walter Zenga helplessly watching.

Ten minutes later the dream of victory which had blossomed
with that goal seemed to be killed when the marvellous Altobelli
took a pass from Liam Brady and shot past McCloy.

Yet it was not a night when Rangers were ready to lie down.
The storming messages from Wallace which had lifted them
down at Turnberry echoed in the players' ears again as they
stormed back. Exactly one minute after what the Italians felt
was the killer goal, Iain Ferguson hammered in a twenty-yard
shot to push Rangers in front once more.

And then, as Rangers dominated the game with powerful
attacking play, it was Ferguson who scored again ten minutes
after half time. Swedish midfield man Robert Prytz made this
chance for Ferguson to score a brave goal and the Italians knew
that they faced the prospect of a humiliating defeat!

They knew, just as everyone in the stadium knew, that

another goal for the Scots would send the game into extra time. And it was clear that if that happened the Rangers team would be the stronger. But with Ferguson having to limp off injured their scoring chances became fewer and Inter survived to go into the draw for the next round.

For Rangers, though, it was a night of glory as the players received a standing ovation from the fans. The disaster of that first leg had been avenged just as Jock Wallace had promised it would be. While they were out of Europe for another season they had proved to the fans, and to themselves, that even the best teams in Europe had to fear and respect Rangers if they were drawn against them.

For Inter the story was different. They were flayed by the Italian press, and club directors too were angry that the team should have flirted so dangerously with a defeat which would have cost them hundreds of thousands of pounds in lost gate receipts. The main target for the blasts of criticism was Karl Heinz Rummenigge who had promised the fans he would score in the second leg and had failed to do so.

For Jock Wallace, of course, the day after the game was spent looking back at the chance Ally McCoist missed in Milan – a goal from that first leg would have been so vital. It was also spent contemplating the fact that he had been proved right by his team's performance.

He admitted: 'There is some satisfaction to be gained from the way the team played but I still think we could have won. People didn't believe me but I knew that a good, honest, old-fashioned British type performance would upset them. Iain Ferguson was magnificent and if he hadn't been injured it might have been us heading into the draw for the third round!

'That's the disappointing thing for me. I did want to have a good run in Europe and in the UEFA Cup the extra round which comes in would have given us the benefit of experience for the players. But at least we know that we can play at the highest level. The Bohemians game didn't give us much in the way of real European experience. But this game against Inter did. If you play the top Italians then you must learn something. They are always so difficult to beat and that League has some of the best players in the world playing in it. Competing with them and holding your own gives us a guideline for the future. And some encouragement too. We didn't do too badly. . . .'

Inter, flying back to Milan, knew that better than anyone. The highly paid soccer aristocrats had been brought back to earth!

I'LL DO IT MY WAY SAYS JOCK WALLACE

Since returning to Rangers as manager in the autumn of 1984 Jock Wallace has brought two League Cups into the Ibrox trophy room. But, still, the League Championship, the ultimate test for any team, has eluded him.

Last season a disastrous run in the Premier League saw Rangers finish up in fourth place with any challenge they might have mounted fading with a defeat from Celtic on New Year's Day.

In this interview with editor Ken Gallacher, Wallace looks back at the season of lost opportunities in the League. He also tells of the team he would like to build at Ibrox and gives the

Rival managers Jock Wallace and Dundee United's Jim McLean share the two Cups at stake before the final. Wallace holds the League Cup while McLean has the Skol Cup in his hands . . . but forty-eight hours later both were in the Ibrox trophy room!

major reason why Northern Ireland international John McClelland was allowed to leave the club and join English First Division side Watford.

The hard hitting Ibrox boss talks about his biggest disappointments in the season – and reveals the demands he makes on his players.

GALLACHER: How disappointed were you about the way the challenge in the League seemed to just peter out around New Year?

WALLACE: I wasn't just disappointed at the way things went after New Year – I was disappointed from the very beginning of our League campaign! We dropped points at home against both St Mirren and Celtic and that was not good enough for any team which is supposed to harbour the ambition of taking the title. I felt then that things weren't right. OK Pat Bonner had a great game against us for Celtic. He was their hero that day but we also missed chances just as we missed them against St Mirren – and as we consistently missed them throughout the season.

Once we started to miss them, one or two of the players began to lose confidence and the pressures got to them. Then, as you say, it all petered out when we lost to Celtic at Ibrox on New Year's Day.

GALLACHER: If you had won that match you would have been within touching distance of Aberdeen, in contention again wouldn't you?

WALLACE: That's how I saw it at the time. But because we lost the game we were suddenly well adrift of both Aberdeen and Celtic. But the League troubles started way back at the start of the season. It wasn't just at New Year that we picked up the problems.

You must never forget that League championships are won over thirty-six games You have to start off with the right attitude and you have to keep that attitude all the way through. There is no way on earth that you can start off badly and expect to be there at the end of the day. You have to start off winning games and keep on winning them until the end of the season. Aberdeen started off well and they never looked back. OK, they had their upset in the League Cup against Airdrie – but in the League they were in control from the very first day. That's the way to win titles. . . .

GALLACHER: Do you think that the slump in the second half of the season came because the players maybe felt they were jinxed in the League? That, after the Celtic game, they just couldn't see themselves taking the title?

Davie Cooper in World Cup action against Iceland – his international
career was restored after a talk with Wallace

WALLACE: I can understand you asking that question but I don't think that was the case. They are professional players and they have to live game by game and I don't think jinxes or anything like that come into it.

Certainly after the Celtic game the League was well beyond our reach but you have to remember that we had a lot of injuries then too. The only player who was free of injuries right through the season was Davie Cooper. Every other player on the books had knocks at one time or another. Even the goalkeepers were hit by that injury run. At one stage of the season we had only one fit goalkeeper on the books to cover the two teams. It was incredible. I'm not making excuses. That's not my way. I wouldn't use the injuries as an excuse for the League performances. You have to get on with the job with whatever players you have available.

Youngster Derek Ferguson, one of the players Wallace is tipping for stardom from the Ibrox youth scheme

GALLACHER: But it did lead to a lack of continuity in your team selections.

WALLACE: Obviously that's the case and it was hard for me because I believe in a settled team. Unfortunately, as well as the injuries, the new players we brought to the club didn't settle in as quickly as I would have liked. Hopefully they will adjust better now and will be able to cope with the pressures of playing for Rangers. These pressures are much greater at Ibrox than they are at most other places, especially when the team is not going as well as the fans want it to go. That makes it more difficult for players coming into the side.

GALLACHER: Ideally you would use how many players in a season . . . maybe eighteen or so?

WALLACE: Less than that if possible. If you look at the top teams in England, say Everton and Liverpool and Manchester United, you'll find that their line-ups are settled. They don't chop and change week after week as we were forced to do last season. We used over thirty players, and you don't win titles when you use that many players.

It goes without saying that you need to have a settled team as early as possible in the season. Remember that the injuries started in the close season when Bobby Williamson broke his leg in Australia. That was a blow because I felt that he and Ally McCoist could team up up front with Iain Ferguson adding his goal-getting ability by coming in from the right side. Fergie is a goal stealer rather than a goal worker if you know what I mean. So it was a blow when we lost Bobby.

And then we had to sell John McClelland which meant shuffling the defence again at a time when we didn't need that kind of problem.

GALLACHER: You were criticised for selling McClelland but he didn't want to play for the club did he?

WALLACE: John McClelland did not want to play for Rangers at the end. He wanted away and he went away. I still believe that the player didn't want to play for the club. And no matter who he is any player who does not want to play for Rangers can go.

As far as I'm concerned it's an article of faith that the players at Ibrox want to play for Rangers above any other club. It has to be that way. It has always been that way and as long as I'm manager it will always be that way.

In fact whether I'm manager or not I'm quite sure that will continue as the policy of the club. Rangers are bigger than any individual, whether it be the chairman, the directors, players, managers or fans . . . the club is the most important thing.

GALLACHER: Apart from the disappointing League form what other disappointments did you have during the season?
WALLACE: Getting knocked out of the Scottish Cup by Dundee was a bitter blow for me. That, plus the defeat from Inter Milan were the worst games for me during the season. I felt all along that we could beat Inter and, in fact, I still believe that we played the right kind of game over there. We were patient and disciplined and we gave them problems. But, at the end of the day we lost two silly goals. Two of their three goals were caused by mistakes that we made and shouldn't have made. Plus the old story of missed chances. Ally McCoist had the best chance of the game and failed to score. If that had gone in then we would have gone through. I'm convinced of that.

But these were the two major let downs for me personally. The Inter game because it meant that we had been knocked out of Europe early when I wanted to have a run in the UEFA Cup to give some of the younger players valuable experience. And the Dundee game because I wanted to be back at Hampden to give the fans something to cheer about at the end of the season.

When we went out of the Scottish Cup the season was over for the fans. We were out of the League race, so there was nothing to play for. And I was sure that we could do well in the Cup last season.

The lads coped well with Morton on a tricky ground in the first round. I was off ill then but I knew how dangerous that match was. The ground was frozen solid and that's not a situation you welcome when you are playing in a sudden death tournament like the Cup. Still, they drew the first game and went on to win the replay comfortably at Ibrox. So it looked to me as if we would be on course for Hampden and our second final of the season. But it wasn't to be. Dundee, who had knocked us out the season before, did it again. There's no way that I want a repeat of that in the future. I want our season to be meaningful right to the death. The fans deserve that from us.

GALLACHER: What were the season's plus factors for you?
WALLACE: Winning the Skol Cup was one of them. We had won it the year before when we defeated Celtic and this time we were able to do it again when we beat Dundee United. We deserved to win because our tactics were right for the day and we scored a marvellous goal through Iain Ferguson. So, taking another Cup to Ibrox was a high spot.

But, as well as that, there were a few plusses from the way young players began to show. In the early part of the season young Derek Ferguson showed his ability in the midfield and

Striker Iain Ferguson, bought by Wallace in the close season, carries the ball clear of this challenge from Hibs' Erich Schaedler. But Ferguson needs time to adjust to the demands made on Rangers players, says the Boss

then right at the death we saw the advent of Ian Durrant who is a cracking midfield player. I'm not suggesting that you can hang all your hopes on these two youngsters right through a season as hard as we get in the Premier League. But I expect both of them to make big bids to force their way into the first team and then stay there.

And I can see Hugh Burns doing that as well. I expect him to consolidate over the two seasons. He has matured a lot. He had a great tour in Australia and then he was outstanding in the Under-21 international in Spain. But, to be honest, he lost his way a little bit last year, the way a lot of young players do. We had to work on him and be very firm with him and make him into a better professional. He has to be more disciplined but he has shown, particularly towards the end of the season, that he can play in the first team.

Dave McPherson has come through well, too. The same goes for him as for Hugh Burns – he has to be that little bit more professional in his approach. Once he gets that right then he could be an outstanding player for Rangers and possibly for Scotland.

He is halfway through his apprenticeship and over the next two years I expect to see him turn into a thorough professional. He showed signs of it during the League Cup final when he did a marvellous marking job on Paul Sturrock and finished up being named Man of the Match – but he's not consistent enough. You have to be able to do that thirty or thirty-five times a year.

GALLACHER: It's back to consistency again then, isn't it?

WALLACE: Of course it is. And you can only achieve it in time with teaching and coaching. It takes a lot of patience. You have to keep the players on the hard road . . . it's easy to take the easy road. Some of them will try that, but it's only by going down the hard road that they can become the kind of professional footballer that Rangers want.

GALLACHER: How different is that, in the light of what you are saying, from what other clubs look for? How difficult is it for players to adapt to the pressures of being at Ibrox?

WALLACE: It is much more difficult than it would be at most other places. Take wee Tommy McLean who was the best crosser of a ball you would ever see. Yet it took him time to settle into the Rangers way of things. I think it is harder for any player who plays for the Old Firm teams, either ourselves or Celtic, because the spotlight is on them all the time. It's not the playing that is any different – it's trying to accept the pressures that go with being a Rangers player. Some lads don't come to terms with it at all. Others take time to build the confidence required to make it at Ibrox.

GALLACHER: Take Cammy Fraser, for example, he looked a confident kind of player when he was with Dundee. But his first season at Ibrox was disappointing even though you did make him captain for a spell. Why was that?

WALLACE: I think the demands made on the player affected him. There are demands made on concentration and confidence, even demands which move into your private life. I think Sandy

Clark said it for most of the players when he left to go to Hearts. He had been around a little bit with Airdrie up here and with West Ham and he admitted when he moved that there wasn't the same pressure at Hearts. He could relax again and enjoy the game whereas he might have been trying too hard with us. But the players have to overcome these problems whether the fans are giving them stick or not – they have to beat it. They have to draw on their own resources, on their own strength and their own courage and their own character to come through the problems and show us what they can do.

It isn't easy and I know that. But if they can come through and believe in themselves then the rewards are tremendous for them. But they have to have this self-belief.

GALLACHER: Is there any player who typifies that for you, a player who can set an example for some of the others?

WALLACE: Davie Cooper epitomises what I am talking about. He believes in his own ability. Maybe he isn't always turning it on, maybe he has a bad game now and then, but he still believes in himself. And right now the fans are with him. He had the wrath of the fans for years. They were on his back

Below left: Another of Wallace's buys – personality forward Ted McMinn who came from Queen of the South where Liverpool had been watching him!

Below right: Hugh Burns, another youngster who is breaking through, challenges Celtic powerhouse Roy Aitken in the air during the 1–1 draw at Parkhead at the end of the season

All Rangers sweeper Dave McPherson needs to hit the big time is
'consistency' says manager Jock Wallace

and they called him the 'Moody Blue' and all the rest of it . . .
but they can't do that now because Davie just goes out there
and plays. And if it doesn't come off for him the first time he
tries to go past the full back and tries it again the next time
because deep down he KNOWS that he can do it.

GALLACHER: Has playing for Scotland in the World Cup
games helped his confidence do you think?

WALLACE: I think so. I had a chat with Davie last season
and I told him straight that he was a great player going nowhere.
He didn't want to play for Scotland, he didn't have any appetite
for it but now he is a recognized international player. But he
has wasted years and you never get those years back. If you
don't listen and learn as a young player then you can lose out.
You have wasted time and there's Davie now, at twenty-nine,
with only a handful of caps when he should have had so many
more.

GALLACHER: I know that you helped persuade him to play
for Scotland again. What did you say to him?

WALLACE: I told him that Johan Cruyff was probably the
greatest player I'd seen and that he always wanted to play for
his country. Cruyff loved playing for Holland and it's there on
the international stage that you make big reputations. Davie
Cooper should have been there in Spain in the last World Cup
finals but he wasn't because he wasn't interested. Now he has
the interest back, the appetite back and I hope he will be in
Mexico.

GALLACHER: To move back to the Premier League for a
moment and the poor form shown by the team there. How upset
were you personally that you didn't mount a real challenge for
the title?

WALLACE: I came back from Australia in the summer
worrying about how we would miss Williamson but still I really
fancied our chances in the League. I honestly believed that we
would be serious contenders right until the death. They are
good players but they simply lost their confidence after one or
two results went against them.

GALLACHER: What caused that do you think?

WALLACE: There could be several factors at work. It could
be down to personality, or maybe being driven too hard or
maybe getting depressed over the criticism they were getting
from the media. It could be any of these things or all of them.

But it's up to them, they have to overcome that. It's not going
to change suddenly. If you want success you have to earn it –
it doesn't come on a plate.

GALLACHER: Is the title still your major aim?

WALLACE: It has to be. Winning the League is the most important thing, more important than success in Europe, and I see the competition getting fiercer and fiercer every year.

GALLACHER: Do you find the Premier League more difficult now than it was before you left Rangers to go to Leicester in 1978?

WALLACE: It's been more difficult for Rangers because we haven't had a settled team. Before I left we were playing just about the same side week after week. I didn't have to use a lot of players then at all and, as I said earlier, this is the mark of any successful side. So that has made it harder.

But in a general sense it is more difficult because Aberdeen and Dundee United have emerged as teams who can win the title and Celtic are always a threat and then last season we saw Dundee come away strongly in the second half of the programme.

In general, the standard is higher. The tactical approach is better and the way things are up here, with the high level of play in the Top Ten, I can see more success coming for Scottish clubs in Europe. Because we are being honed to a real competitive edge in every game. There isn't an easy game in the Premier League nowadays!

GALLACHER: Apart from the 'settled' look you want to the team, what else do Rangers need to come close to the title?

WALLACE: We need players who will accept responsibility. Quite honestly last year there were too many players in the team who would not accept responsibility for their own jobs, far less for other people's jobs.

In the team I had before we had players like John Greig and Alex MacDonald, Sandy Jardine and Derek Johnstone and Tommy McLean – all of them were shouters on the park. They passed on advice, they kept people on their toes. All of them kept at it out there on the field shouting and advising and moaning and encouraging – and always accepting responsibility. When I brought young players into the team then it was easy for them. All they had to do was run and pass and LISTEN. Because all of these players who were shouting on the field had been over the course. They had come through the dark days when the team wasn't lifting Leagues and Cups and they had gone through all that pain and emerged better players. We have to have players who can do that, players who can help their team-mates through a hard time on the field. And still do their own jobs. That's what I am aiming for, that kind of team.

I said when I came here it would take three years to build my own team. I'm not saying that team will definitely win

Another of the 'new boys' who went through a settling-in period after he joined Rangers – here Cammy Fraser gets in a shot against St Mirren despite a challenge from Mark Fulton

League championships because there are other guys building teams. But by that time it will be my OWN team. We're well along the road to getting that team now.

GALLACHER: Ideally what kind of team would you like to create here? Do you have any type of side in mind for that three-year plan?

WALLACE: I think Everton is the kind of team I'd like to have. The way they performed last year, the way their players battled through that season to come out with two major trophies and just miss a third was something special. That was a performance!

They have honest players playing for each other. That honesty is the greatest quality that they have for me. That is what can carry teams through difficult times . . . and it was good to see that kind of honesty being rewarded.

I think that Peter Reid, their midfield player, says what life is about in football. He was out of the team, suffered injuries and fought his way back and he knows what life is all about now. I don't know the man but he is the kind of professional I would like to handle. You're talking about a man who has been resurrected. He plays with conviction and he obviously has the ability to lift the players round about him. He is a very influential player and a very honest player.

And I admire the way Andy Gray has come back. He has realized that you have to work hard and he has done that. Again he has learned to accept responsibility and it's when you do that you become a top professional.

GALLACHER: Can you get that over to experienced players or is it better to teach these lessons to youngsters.

WALLACE: The earlier that they learn the better it is for them. The youth policy we are pursuing at Ibrox sees about forty kids a week coming in to play trials and to train and we will be stepping that up in the months to come.

But you can get the message over to anyone who is prepared to listen and to learn. Listen and learn – that's the secret. That's what it was when I was a kid at Airdrie and then down south

Former Rangers defender John McClelland in action for his country, Northern Ireland. Wallace says he did not want to play for Rangers

at West Brom and it's still the same today. You learned from your manager or your coach or the older players and if you were prepared to listen to them then you were on the road to becoming a better player. But there is no short cut – you have to work hard to be a professional. You have to take the knocks and then get up and get on with the job. There is no use sitting around moping. You wouldn't catch someone like Peter Reid feeling sorry for himself – he would fight on until he broke through. That's what I want my players to do.

Striker Sandy Clark who moved to Hearts from Ibrox and admitted there was so much less pressure at Tynecastle

GALLACHER: You've said how important the youth policy is, could you go into that a little more?

WALLACE: We have intensified the whole youth programme this year. We had an Under-14 team doing very well, the Under-15 team has done not too badly and the Under-16 team we left a bit late but we have one player through from there already. A young lad called Angus McPherson whom I quite like and who has chances. He will be on the groundstaff in the new season.

We have had a tremendous amount of trials at Ibrox all through the season trying to find the laddies that we want. It's a lot of work, just about every night of the week at times, but it has to be done because that is where the future of the club lies. If we can get the same success rate over the next few years as we are seeing now from the likes of Derek Ferguson, Ian Durrant, Davie McFarlane and Hugh Burns then we will be all right. The first three were in the Scotland Under-18 team and they have been impressive there, as well as for us.

As I pointed out earlier we are well along the road to getting the kind of team I want, and we will need it because the competition is going to be fiercer and the game itself in Scotland is getting faster every season. I had a spell in England with Leicester so believe me when I tell you that the standard of fitness among the top Scottish clubs is higher than it is in the First Division down there. Our clubs train harder, I'm not saying that we are all better football players but we are fitter because we work harder.

GALLACHER: Finally, what signs should we look for in players to see how far along the road to success they have travelled?

WALLACE: Look for honesty from them. Look for confidence. Look for responsibility. All of these things are being drummed into them and given time they will see what we are driving at on that training ground day after day. It's close to coming right. We played at Chelsea at the end of the season and the confidence was showing there. Ally McCoist finished the season on a high. Other players were looking good. I took that as a sign of better times. I don't think you'll see Rangers as far away from the title as they were last season . . . we won't be giving up as easily as we did before.

When we can bring in performances like those against Dundee United and Inter Milan more consistently then we will be in at the death. The players have shown in those games what they can achieve – all they have to do is provide that commitment and that concentration a lot more often. Then I'll be happy!

CHEERS TO THE SKOL CUP

The contrast in European results between Dundee United and Rangers seemed a crucial factor in the build-up to the final of the Skol Cup. That, plus the more impressive path to the tournament final carved out by the Tannadice men, encouraged a belief that, at last, United would end their jinx run against Rangers.

The man who took the League Cup to Ibrox – striker Iain Ferguson whose goal beat Dundee United at Hampden. Here is the all-action Ferguson who set Hampden alight as he collected his first ever medal

Beforehand the rival skippers Craig Paterson and Dundee United's
Paul Hegarty share the trophies. Afterwards Hegarty summed it all up
when he said: 'I'm afraid that Rangers have done it to us again . . .'

For not once in the history of the Tannadice club had they
ever beaten Rangers in a major Cup competition. Nor had they
won any of their trophies by playing in the final at Hampden.

They had won the League Cup (now re-named the Skol
League Cup after a sponsorship deal) twice, both times at Dens
Park in Dundee. The first time they defeated Aberdeen, and
the second time around they beat their same street city rivals
Dundee.

Rangers, of course, had always been a jinx team to Jim
McLean's men. Over the years the hard-working Tannadice
boss had admitted that his team failed too often when they came
up against the Ibrox men. Originally it seemed to be a Glasgow
jinx. Gradually, though, McLean's men began to pick up more
and more points when they faced Celtic. Rangers remained their
bogey!

Of course, McLean and his players maintained confidently
that records were there to be broken, bogeys to be laid to rest
and that, on form, they were capable of lifting the trophy for
the third time inside four years.

They were bolstered by a magnificent European performance.
Playing in the same tournament as Rangers, the UEFA Cup,
they travelled to Linz in Austria and returned home with a 2–1
win. Goals from Eamonn Bannon and Billy Kirkwood had given

70

them that result while Rangers had struggled in Italy, losing three goals to Inter Milan. These, then, were the contrasting fortunes of the two teams just days before the Sunday shoot out at Hampden which was to decide the destination of the first major trophy of the season.

The trophy had been given a fresh format after criticisms of the unwieldly structure favoured the season before when the competition dragged on into spring before Rangers beat Celtic in an Old Firm final.

This time the League had opted for a short sharp knock-out competition. . .one which the clubs favoured, the sponsors welcomed, and the fans wanted. Only the semi-final ties were to be on a home and away basis. The rest of the tournament would be straight knock-out with the rabbits having every chance to defeat the giants – as Airdrie showed in the very first round when they knocked out Aberdeen at Broomfield.

So the message was plain to the big guns after that shock

The winning Rangers team with their trophies and their medals celebrate at Hampden. The players are, back row left to right: Ally Dawson, Dave Mitchell, Peter McCloy, Ian Redford, Iain Ferguson, Ally McCoist and John McClelland; front row left to right: Robert Russell, Davie Cooper, Cammy Fraser, Craig Paterson, Dave McPherson and Robert Prytz

opening in the tournament by former Scotland boss Ally MacLeod's part-timers at Airdrie. They had all been warned and while Rangers and Dundee United moved into the second round of the competition with home draws, the Tannadice men already, that early, looked the more convincing of the two teams.

They disposed of local rivals Forfar, a First Division team many thought would make things hard for McLean's men, by five goals, shared by Eamonn Bannon, Paul Sturrock and John Reilly with one goal each, and close-season signing Stuart Beedie with a couple.

Meanwhile at Ibrox, Rangers struggled to defeat Falkirk, assistant manager Alex Totten's old team. A goal from Davie McPherson brought them the reward of another home draw against Raith Rovers. This time their progress was more comfortable with Craig Paterson, Ian Redford and two goal Ally McCoist combining to please the ten thousand fans who were at Ibrox for the game.

United had had to travel to play at Boghead against the Premier League new boys Dumbarton. On paper it was a tie which might have been awkward – especially remembering the new sudden-death format of the tournament. But there were no signs of nerves from Ralph Milne and Davie Dodds who scored two goals each in the so-convincing 4–0 win. That brought them to their biggest test – a clash with Celtic, though it was a home tie.

Rangers, meanwhile were asked to travel to Central Park to meet Cowdenbeath where former Celtic defender and assistant manager John Clark had taken over. Clark had guided the little Fife club to two shock wins – over First Division Partick Thistle and Premier League St Mirren. Both matches had been on their own ground and Clark relished the idea of tangling there with the team which had been his greatest rival over the years he had spent at Parkhead.

It was a plum tie for the Fifers, a challenge for Clark and a problem for Rangers after the earlier results they had achieved.

But United had the bigger problem and it took them until extra time before they could subdue Celtic who were still chasing their first trophy win under manager Davie Hay.

A sell-out crowd at Tannadice where the gates were shut before the teams kicked off saw a fascinating struggle.

International striker Paul Sturrock scored first for United but after Celtic had equalised to send the game into extra time it was substitute youngster John Clark who snatched a spectacular winner – a goal which carried his team into the semi-finals.

Rangers didn't need extra time at Cowdenbeath. They won

comfortably against the trophy's giant killers with goals from their new signing Iain Ferguson plus others from Ian Redford and Robert Russell giving them a 3–1 win.

When the draw was made for the semi-finals – and now the games became two-legged affairs – United were paired with yet another Premier League outfit. Following Dumbarton and Celtic they were now asked to meet Hearts.

Rangers, still to meet one side from the top division, were drawn against tiny Meadowbank Thistle. Again the part-timers here had become giant killers in the competition and two Premier League clubs had failed against them. Their first scalp was Morton who were beaten 2–1 and then they went on to beat their capital rivals Hibs by the same score after extra time.

It was obvious that the men from Meadowbank could not be taken lightly – but equally obvious that, with the semi-final being played over two legs, Rangers would find it easier than Morton and Hibs had done. When Meadowbank had to change their home venue to Tynecastle, things looked even rosier for the Ibrox side.

Basically, however, the damage to Meadowbank was done at Ibrox in the first-leg game. That is where their dreams of glory

On their way to the final, Rangers disposed of Meadowbank Thistle in the two-legged semi-final. Striker Ally McCoist is seen in action here against the little Edinburgh team in the 4–0 win at Ibrox

An earlier clash between the Skol Cup finalists has Scottish
international team-mates Davie Cooper and Maurice Malpas in a
touchline confrontation while Eamonn Bannon awaits the outcome

were destroyed as thirteen thousand fans saw Rangers coast to
a 4–0 win with goals from Cammy Fraser, Iain Ferguson and
two from Ally McCoist, the tournament's top marksman.

On paper the tie was over. In reality there was no way that
Meadowbank could come back. But they did salvage some kind
of memories for themselves when they drew the second-leg game
at Tynecastle. Only a goal from Ally McCoist saved Rangers
from an embarrassing defeat.

United should have found it much harder against Hearts but,
by now, the Tannadice team were showing the Cup form which
was to follow them into the Scottish Cup later in the season.
Although Hearts had progressed solidly through the tournament
and had beaten United's city rivals Dundee in the previous
round they couldn't match the Tannadice men in either of the
two games.

Young John Clark, scourge of Celtic in the quarter-finals,
repeated his match-winning act in the opening clash between

the teams at Tynecastle. He scored both goals there in United's 2–1 win. That set United on the road for Hampden, but a convincing 3–1 victory at their own Tannadice made certain that they were the team who would face Rangers – and would do it with confidence. This was the third Premier League club they had defeated and the goals from Bannon, Billy Kirkwood and Dodds gave them a much more impressive look than Rangers in the march to the final.

It was not the fault of the Ibrox club that they had been drawn against weaker opposition. Nevertheless the way United had disposed of Dumbarton, Celtic and Hearts gave them an undoubted edge over their Glasgow rivals.

Then, when the European ties were played just a few days before the final, the belief of the Tannadice players and fans that this was to be the year they would lay their Rangers jinx, was reinforced still further.

Rangers seemed up against it. But there is always that old adage in Scottish soccer which says that Rangers are never more dangerous than when they look down and out. No rival manager likes to go in against an Ibrox side which has been written off. . .Dundee United's Jim McLean was no exception.

While admitting how well his team had played in Austria, McLean was not ready to forecast that they would win the Skol trophy.

Returning from Linz he said: 'That was one of our best ever performances abroad. We didn't have a bad player. Now I have to think about who to leave out for the final against Rangers.

'One thing is certain we will need the same motivation we showed in Austria if we are to beat Rangers and take the Cup. Our result in Linz won't make any difference. Nor will the fact that Rangers lost in Italy. This is a different game and all of us have to realize that and get our attitude right before meeting Rangers.'

That was the major theme from McLean as he prepared his team for the Sunday shoot-out which was to be televised live throughout Scotland. He reckoned that his team were capable of taking the trophy again – for the third time in four years – but he knew, too, that their attitude had to be exactly right. If it wasn't, they would fail yet again as they faced up to the side which had proved to be their biggest jinx down the years.

A year earlier in the semi-final of the same tournament Rangers had beaten United and gone on to win the Cup. And in the 1981–82 final Rangers had beaten them 2–1 and now the Ibrox team were aiming to win the trophy for a record tenth time.

In their previous meeting in the final, Rangers had stopped United taking the Cup for the third year in succession – and they had come back from being a goal down to do it. That was the only time in the previous five finals that a team had come from behind to clinch victory. Rangers fans took delight in pointing out this fact as they taunted United supporters over their inability to beat the Ibrox men in a Cup tournament.

As well as that Cup problem, United had lost 1–0 to Rangers in their only previous meeting of the season. That was at Ibrox when the solitary goal of the game was scored by Craig Paterson, the Rangers skipper and centre half.

But as the countdown came the rival managers ignored the past and concentrated on the present. . . .

At a face to face meeting at Hampden forty-eight hours before the game they agreed that the final would be a showpiece for attacking football. Boomed Jock Wallace: 'We don't know any other way to play. Our supporters demand that we attack, demand that we go forward and demand that we win. When it comes to a final then they want us to go after that trophy as hard as we know how. This won't be any different. We lost in Italy against Inter Milan but I didn't blame the players for that. They did well against a very good team. Now they have the chance to come back quickly. And successfully. . . .'

As Wallace was laying his battle plans and taking his team to Turnberry for their final training stints, McLean, more low key, was also promising to attack.

'The only way to beat Rangers is to go at them,' he stressed. 'If we can be a bit daring then we can win the match and take the trophy back to Dundee. Basically we are good enough to do that. The players have the skill and the experience to win the game but they must do themselves justice at Hampden.

'Honestly, if we do that and if we attack as we can then with the players we have I don't see us losing to Rangers.'

McLean sounded more confident than usual. It was as if his side's experiences in Europe had added an extra dimension to their play and to their off-field attitude.

So the stage was set and forty-five thousand fans ignored the live television broadcast to travel to Hampden and savour the occasion. A huge Rangers support was there outnumbering the tangerine clad crowds who had journeyed from Dundee to see if their side could claim the first trophy of the season. . . .

Unhappily it was not a game which lived up to the pre-match expectations of the two team bosses. Nor to the expectations of most of us who relished the thought of an attacking classic. It was tough and it was dour and it was tense. The prize seemed to mean so much to the two sets of players that no one was willing to run the risk of making a mistake which could cost his team the chance of glory.

There were five bookings in the game as Scotland's top referee Brian McGinlay fought hard to keep a tight grip on things. It was to his credit that he maintained discipline as the teams battled it out bruisingly on the field. Robert Russell, Dave McPherson and Davie Cooper of Rangers and Paul Hegarty and Richard Gough of Dundee United were all shown the yellow card.

But if that tarnished the game for the five men who fell foul of McGinlay the glory belonged to Rangers. And especially to three of their players. . . .

The first was close-season signing Iain Ferguson the blond striker who grabbed the only goal of the game to make sure that the two trophies would take their place in the historic Ibrox trophy room. The original League Cup and the new Skol Cup were both there to be won and Fergie's goal was enough to

Below left: Robert Russell who came close for Rangers in the first half of the Hampden final against Dundee United

Below right: Rangers skipper Craig Paterson, the man who collected their only trophy last season as the Ibrox side retained their hold on the League Cup

make Rangers record winners of the first and the first winners of the second.

It arrived just a minute before half time after an opening half which had seen the two teams spar cautiously and carefully with only two chances to excite the crowd. These tries came from Robert Russell of Rangers and Eamonn Bannon of Dundee United but neither could match the finishing style of Ferguson who had been left out of the Rangers team in the midweek European clash in the San Siro Stadium in Milan!

It was a good build-up to that so vital goal. Davie Cooper started things off with a pass to Russell. On the ball went to Ian Redford who in turn moved it in to Ferguson. The striker's shot swept past veteran Hamish McAlpine and into the net.

Afterwards a jubilant Ferguson grinned: 'That was easily the best moment I've had since joining up with Rangers in the summer. I said when I left Dundee to come to Ibrox that I wanted to taste success in the game. Well, here we are just part of the way through the season and I've won my first medal. I feel great about that and I feel great about the goal. . . .

'I was surprised to find that much space when the ball came to me. It wasn't easy getting into space out there today and I didn't have a lot of time to think before shooting for goal.

'It's really good because I have been left out a couple of times and that disappointed me. It's not always easy to fit into a new team and a lot is expected of players with Rangers.'

But not much more than the winning goal in a Cup final

Ally McCoist is en route to being the tournament's top scorer as he nets this one against Meadowbank Thistle in the Ibrox semi-final

could be expected of anyone! Especially since the goal meant that Rangers qualified for Europe as tournament winners and it helped erase the memory of the defeat in Milan so quickly after that Italian flop.

The second player who was celebrating the win with extra verve was Ally McCoist because his goal scoring achievements in the tournament – he scored five times – meant that he was the Skol Cup's number one goal getter. That won him a £1,000 holiday for two in the Caribbean!

And the third player who shared in some extra glory was young 'sweeper' Dave McPherson. He had been asked to combat the menace of United's gifted striker Paul Sturrock. And McPherson, still inexperienced compared to his international opponent, won that duel hands down. So much so that Sturrock scarcely threatened the Rangers goal in the entire ninety minutes and McPherson was voted Man of the Match and given a gold lager tankard to go alongside his winner's medal.

But, of course, for the Tannadice team it was a day of misery. A day when their old jinx struck again. Once more they had failed to beat Rangers in a major Cup competition. Once more they had to make the long sad trek back to Tannadice without a trophy after a Hampden appearance.

Skipper Paul Hegarty's words seemed to sum up their afternoon: 'I'm afraid that Rangers have done it to us again. . . .'

Those ten words said it all. Rangers had, indeed, done it again. While Jim McLean thought his side had deserved more from the game the victory had gone to the team who had been able to finish lethally.

There were times when United had played polished possession football but no one struck for goal the way that Iain Ferguson had done. That was the essential difference between the two sides. That and the hunger which always drives on Rangers teams when they reach Hampden. They went onto the field that Sunday afternoon determined to prove to everyone in Scotland that they could bounce back after the disappointment of San Siro. Determined, too, to prove that they were good enough to retain the trophy they had taken the previous season in an extra-time drama against Old Firm rivals Celtic.

This time they won it more easily and as Jock Wallace said: 'I never felt we were in any danger even though United had a lot of possession. It was a great, great goal and we deserved it.'

And so, while the rest of the season proved to be an anti-climax, Rangers did have something to celebrate. A record-breaking trophy win which made sure of that European competition place the following season!

SO GLAD TO BE BACK
by Derek Johnstone

People have always maintained that there is something special about playing for Rangers. All my life I've been told that but it took a transfer to Chelsea to really bring it home to me. . . .

Now I know that it is true. Not in any way does Derek Johnstone of Chelsea even have the same ring to it as Derek Johnstone of Rangers. Don't think because I'm saying that now that I'm having a go at Chelsea or at English football, because I'm not. The one message I'm hoping to get over is that Rangers Football Club is a very special team to be a part of.

It was a wrench when I left and I suppose in a way it was a mistake because I knew deep down that I wouldn't be happy anywhere else in the game. After all I'd spent half of my life as a Rangers player. Remember I joined the club when I was just fifteen years old. I played in an Old Firm final when I was sixteen and scored the only goal that day to give us the League Cup win we had wanted so much.

How could any other club take Rangers' place in my affections after all these years. All these trophy wins. The European Cup Winners' Cup, the two trebles . . . the other Cup wins, all of them were a part of me. And all of them linked me with Rangers for the rest of my life.

At the time I thought it was right to make a break. There were younger players ready to come through. A lot of the players who had been with me in the team had gone. Either they had lost their first team places or else they had moved away to other clubs. And so when it was made clear to me that younger players were to get their chance, I thought it would be a good thing to try my luck in England. Chelsea were the team who came for me and I was delighted to join them. I knew they were ambitious. I knew that they wanted to be among the country's top teams and I still felt that I had enough experience to help them get there.

That it didn't quite work out is really no one's fault. Or if you want to blame anyone then blame the players who were there in front of me and doing a good job for the club by the time I signed.

80

Originally I thought that the Stamford Bridge team would want me to play up front – but Kerry Dixon was there and the goals he was scoring made it impossible to displace him. Then, too, alongside him they had little David Speedie and he was the perfect foil for Kerry. So, end of story – there was no room up front for yours truly.

Of course, I thought, I also have experience playing at the back. After all I'd won Scottish honours there and I'd been centre half with Rangers in the Cup Winner's Cup final when we beat Moscow Dynamo in Barcelona. Also, I reasoned, I'm getting older and so there could be a case for me dropping back into defence again. But Joe McLaughlin who had moved south from Morton was the man in possession there and the way he was playing there was no moving him either.

So for most of the nearly two seasons that I spent at Stamford Bridge I was in the second team or one of the reserves for the League side. I managed a handful of games only. These came when someone was injured. But there was no way that when

Derek Johnstone, third from left, watches team-mate Ian Redford land after sending a flying header towards the Dundee United goal. Also in the picture are United's John Holt and Rangers pair Craig Paterson and Dave McPherson

Kerry Dixon, for instance, was fit again I would keep him out. He had proved himself one of the deadliest scorers in England and the way he has forced himself into Bobby Robson's plans proves just how lethal he can be. Little David Speedie has been the same. OK, he isn't going to score as many goals as Kerry but he is always going to nick a few and he is also going to make openings for whoever is alongside him. He proved against England at Hampden when he made his Scottish debut, that he is as brave as they come and never likely to be overawed by the big occasion. I was really pleased to see him getting that Scottish cap because I thought he deserved it. Watching him play for the first team and playing with him in training it was obvious that some day he would play for his country. And forget about that Yorkshire accent he has – David is as fiercely Scottish as anyone you are likely to meet.

However, that's another story. While David was carving out a Scotland chance and the others were playing at the top of their form I was out in the cold. My own career was heading nowhere fast.

Dundee United moved in to try to sign me. I went up to Tannadice and played for them for a short spell, but I couldn't bring myself to sign for them. It was hard enough to cope with

This low drive by Derek Johnstone is blocked by Dundee United keeper Hamish McAlpine. Johnstone could have joined the Tannadice team from Chelsea, but he says his heart was with Rangers

being away from Rangers while I was down south. Trying to handle that while playing for a Scottish team would have been impossible for me. Yet, funnily enough, United had been the team I supported as a youngster when I was going to school in Dundee. Once, too, they had come close to signing me before I joined Rangers as a full professional. But at that late stage in my career I knew I couldn't play for them, even though I have a tremendous admiration for their manager Jim McLean and the job he has done with the club.

It was just that by that time I knew if I ever returned to Scotland it could only be to Ibrox. There was nothing silly or sentimental about that feeling – it was simply that I realized that I should never have left the club in the first place.

Circumstances forced the move on me to some extent but it wasn't a move that was right for me. And I believe I would have said that even if I'd gone to Chelsea, made the first team and been a success. There is just something about being a Rangers player that is special. It means more than anything else to me.

I suppose, deep down, I always knew that but the exile in England brought it all home to me. When the talk started about Rangers wanting me I pestered the Chelsea club officials to find out if it was true. I told them that it was the one club I wanted to go to, the one club I wanted to play for before my career was over. Eventually they agreed to sell me back to Rangers and I was on my way home again. I don't think I've ever been happier than when I walked back in through that front door, into the marble hallway and up that imposing staircase to sign for the club for the second time.

Possibly the years with Chelsea were wasted as far as my career was concerned. But I did learn how important Rangers had been in my life and now all I want to do is repay the club a little bit for what they have given me over the years.

There has been a big change since I left. Most of my contemporaries have gone. Big Peter McCloy is the only one, really, who is left from the years when we were winning the trebles. Robert Russell and Ally Dawson came in at the end of that side, just as it was breaking up. So there were a whole lot of new faces around the dressing room when I returned towards the end of last season.

And maybe that's where some of the team's problems came from last year. Being a Rangers player is a whole lot different from being a star player with another club, no matter what club you're talking about! There are greater demands made on the players – by the club's constant search for success, by the tradition which exists inside Ibrox, by the hunger and ambition shown by the manager, Jock Wallace, and by the support's need for success. They have been bred on success. Either they have seen the team achieve it themselves or they have been raised on tales of past glories. No matter what it is, or from what direction the pressures are coming, the message is always the same in the end – second best is not good enough for Rangers.

It takes time to get through to players and so, perhaps, last year was difficult for the lads who had just joined the club, or just come into the first team.

Winning the Skol Cup was great – that was before I was back but I celebrated that win as if I was still a Rangers player – and until New Year they stayed within touching distance of the Premier League leaders. But then came the slump, and it was in the middle of that slump that I returned. By then some of the players had lost confidence, the supporters were picking on them, and because of that, I think, morale was low.

Players were unwilling to try things knowing that if a pass went astray or a shot off target then the boo boys would be on top of them. I've suffered from barracking and I know how hard it is to battle through the problems and eventually find your form again. You see, when Rangers are going through a bad patch then every team coming to Ibrox arrives there with one thought in mind. All they want to do is sit back in defence, frustrate us for half an hour or so and then let our own fans turn on us. When that happens the opposition know that they could be on their way to a win. Or at least a draw. Because when the booing starts then nervousness spreads through the team and soon no one is willing to try anything which could be unexpected enough, or imaginative enough, or bold enough, to change the game and stop the jeers.

I know that the fans suffer along with us at times. But I wish that they would simply stay behind the team all the time. If they would do that then some of the younger players would be able to relax a little more when they reach the first team. They would be able to play the game without worrying that a thousand voices are ready to hand out stick immediately anything goes wrong.

Having said that and at the same time hoping that the fans will be more patient, I also accept that it's up to us to get on with the game. Everyone in life has pressures and we have to be able to take the hard times as well as the good. It's just that it's a little harder for the newer players to understand. Some of them aren't used to the demands that are made of Rangers players.

That old ability in the air hasn't deserted Johnstone as he outjumps
Dundee United and Scotland defender Richard Gough

It's not enough to draw against Celtic or Aberdeen or Dundee
United, or anyone else for that matter. You have to go out to
win the game. That's what the fans expect. It's also what the
club has expected right through its long and honour-laden
history!

It takes time to adjust and players need help along the way.
Maybe that's where I can make a contribution off the field for
the club. Even though I've been away for a short spell I am
still one of the most experienced Rangers players at Ibrox and
I am trying to pass on to the other players some of the things
I have picked up in my time with the club.

I've told them that if they can start winning regularly, keeping
up their form in every game and not just in the odd match here
and there, then they can be playing to forty thousand crowds
every week. That's the response they would get – and I don't
think that we are too far away from giving the fans the kind of
team that they want to see. I believe that the Boss is on the

right lines – and remember I've been over the course with him before, in Europe and at home when the team was winning trophies regularly!

He knows what he wants and he will get it. He wants to see a team where players won't lose concentration, where they will battle through off days to get things right for the team, where the lads will all play for each other. It sounds simple but when there is a lack of confidence around then it isn't so easy to achieve. We had that in the team which won two trebles. If one player was having a nightmare then another would be alongside him helping him through, guiding him in the right direction, encouraging him until he was back on song. All the good teams have that kind of team spirit and that is something which we still have to achieve with the current squad.

I'll play anywhere the Boss asks me to play right now, just as long as I can help him achieve his aims. He wants Rangers back on top. And that's where I'd like them to be before I have to retire from the game.

If he wants me up front then I'll play there. But, quite honestly, at this stage of my career it would make more sense to drop back to a deeper position. Either in the back four or playing in a role just in front of the two central defenders. The game up front has changed since the days when I was scoring forty goals in a season. I was a target man, pure and simple. The ball was played up to me and I laid it off or had a go for goal myself. Now teams are playing with runners up front and that was never my strong suit. So, I see my future with the club in a defensive role. I've played there with success for Rangers before and I believe I can do so again. I hope to and I hope it comes together quickly enough to help Rangers win another title.

That has to be the main objective. To win a championship the players have to learn to be consistent. That is the essential quality in any title-winning side.

There are happy signs that a title challenge is coming. Towards the end of last season Ally McCoist began to look the player that Rangers paid all that money for. I think the boy has great ability but like some of the others he was trying too hard at times and his play was suffering. Anyhow, if you look at his last dozen games or so you'll find that he scored in almost every one of them and by the end of the season his confidence was sky high and that is very important when you are a striker.

Then too, we have tremendous young players who are forcing their way into the Premier League side. Derek Ferguson played quite a few games in the first team last season and as captain

Above left: Ian Durrant, a youngster Johnstone tips for the top, moves in to tackle Willie McStay in the Ibrox teenager's first Old Firm game

Above right: Another of Johnstone's players for the future is Derek Ferguson, the little midfield man who was captain of Scotland's Under-18 team last season

of Scotland's Under-18 side he proved himself in European competition as well. I cannot praise him too highly from what I've seen of him. He is going to be an outstanding player and in the near future he will be as important to us as Paul McStay is to Celtic. You watch out for the way Derek develops. . . .

Then there is Ian Durrant who came in for a handful of games at the end of the season. He played against Celtic at Parkhead and was brilliant. Then when we went down to Chelsea for a game in aid of the Bradford Disaster Fund a week after the season finished, he ran the show. Honestly, there he was, just a kid, yet he was in command of that midfield. He has been really impressive.

And these are not the only youngsters around. There's the defender David McFarlane who is also in the Scotland youth team at Under-18 level. Then there are one or two even younger.

Plus we have experienced players like Cammy Fraser and Iain Ferguson who have been at Ibrox for a year and have learned what is required of them. Both will be better players this year, I'm sure of that. It's happened in the past that players have needed time to settle. Both Cammy and Fergie were given stick by some sections of the support last season. Now I'm sure that they will be able to make these fans eat their words. The combination of experience plus the breath of fresh air that really good youngsters bring into any team can lift the Rangers side to the heights that I remember from the teams I was in before.

I accept that it is more difficult now to win the Premier League. Aberdeen and Dundee United have both improved even in the short time I've been away. And Celtic are always a strong threat. No one can look at our League now and suggest that it's a two horse race for the Old Firm. The challenges of the Premier League have changed all of that.

Playing each other four times in the League every season makes it more difficult. And when you think that the top teams can be playing each other again in the two Cup competitions then you can understand the problems. Imagine playing Dundee United five times as we did last season. Obviously players realize the little tricks you can all get up to. They know each other's weaknesses and strengths and managers know the basic tactics which teams use. So more time has to be spent trying to outwit the opposition. That can be hard enough at any time, but when you are doing it four or five times in the one season then it's a major problem. Just take a look at Celtic and Dundee United last year. They met up six times – four games in the League Championship, once in the Skol Cup quarter-finals and then again, in the Scottish Cup final. Could there be anything that they didn't know about each other?

If we can get a good run in Europe this season when you can break free of the restrictions imposed by the competitiveness of the Top Ten, then it will help the team. Playing against the top teams from the Continent is something I've missed in the time I've been away. Some of the great games were against the likes of Juventus, Torino, Bayern Munich, Cologne and the rest. It's my belief that playing in Europe when everyone is living together and training together and spending all their time together away from training helps enormously. You can talk out problems that way. You can build an understanding with team-mates. You can develop the team spirit I talked about earlier.

And if you can do that then you can talk about titles. I'd like another League Championship medal before I retire to add to the three I have already. I'd also like a sixth Scottish Cup medal which would be something really extra special. And I'd like to score at least one more League goal because that would be my hundredth Premier League goal for Rangers.

Let's hope I can get that early in the season and let's hope it won't be the only thing we'll be celebrating. I'm glad to be back – but I want success in the little time I have left!

A RETURN TO DUBLIN BRINGS TROUBLE

There had been a nine year gap between the two games – yet manager Jock Wallace was still able to recall the European Cup clash with Bohemians of Dublin.

Then Rangers won the 'treble' under Wallace and were returning to play in the Continent's number one competition after a gap of a decade. . . .

Now they were returning to play the part-timers of Bohemians in the UEFA Cup and Wallace was back in Europe for the first

The sight which the Dublin side Bohemians feared most of all at Ibrox – winger Davie Cooper in action. Here he moves into the kind of attack which brought Rangers their late, late victory . . .

time since leaving Rangers for Leicester in the summer of 1978.

It was a return Wallace had relished since qualifying for Europe by winning the League Cup against Celtic at Hampden the previous season. He admitted: 'I have missed European football. It's OK to play friendlies now and again but the real cut and thrust of European club competition is vital to any team. And any player. And any manager!'

So perhaps it was with some disappointment – and probably some concern – that Wallace accepted the summer news that in the first round the Ibrox side would be heading for Dublin. Ten years earlier they had played Bohemians and Wallace was struck by a bottle hurled through the window of the Rangers team bus as it went down O'Connell Street after the game.

Now they had to go back and the threat of crowd trouble loomed menacingly over the first-leg tie which was scheduled for the Irish capital.

Wallace would have preferred more glamour in the first leg. But he knew that it would not be an easy game for the Scots. The Bohemians coach Billy Young, the man who was in charge of the Irish side the first time the two clubs met, laughingly admitted before the tie: 'We don't expect to win the UEFA Cup – all we want to do is let the players enjoy themselves!'

But that jokey outlook hid the fact that in seven separate European campaigns only one team, West German cracks Hamburg, had ever beaten them in Dublin. And that was with a late goal. . . .

Even Rangers with their treble-winning team all those years back could only draw 1–1 at Dalymount. Admittedly, then they

It looks like Dave McPherson's goal – but it isn't! Skipper Craig Paterson, half hidden by the powerful challenge from a Bohemians defender (*centre*) is the man whose header flies for goal

had the cushion of a 4–1 lead from the first game at Ibrox. But Bohemians would not make life easy for their more illustrious opponents.

So much for the on-field problems. Those off the field were also causing the Ibrox club headaches. Rangers tried to dissuade their huge travelling support from crossing the Irish Sea. They partly succeeded – but their message was not accepted by the thousands of Rangers fans in Ulster who made the trip over the border of that troubled and divided island.

It was against that background that Wallace tried to prepare his players for the task which faced them. He expected the game to be hard and physical and explained: 'We need a different approach from the type of game we might normally adopt in Europe. If you play Germans or Italians or almost any of the Continental teams then you need poise and discipline and you know that players will be given more time on the ball. That won't apply here and we have to realize it from the beginning.'

While he preached that philosophy to the players Wallace was also worrying over the problems the fans might cause. It was his comeback to Europe and he wanted nothing to spoil the night for him or his beloved Rangers.

As it happened on that September evening in Dublin the return to Europe was wrecked!

On the field the Ibrox men slumped to a 3–2 defeat after twice being in front. . . .

Off the field the fans rioted and put the club's European future in jeopardy. It was even worse than Wallace and his directors had feared. It was a night when the Glasgow club was

Now the ball is in the net as keeper Dermot O'Neill can't reach it in time. McPherson still has the best view with Paterson just catching a glimpse of that vital opener at Ibrox

shamed by their supporters, most of whom had travelled from Northern Ireland for the game.

It was that trouble off the field which overshadowed anything that happened between the two teams.

During the day there had been hints of what could happen. A ferry carrying Glasgow based fans from Liverpool to Dublin was forced to return to the English port after fighting broke out in the two bars aboard. But the worst was reserved for the game and manager Jock Wallace was involved in the thick of things as he tried to get his own fans to behave themselves.

The riot exploded at half time and was sparked off when a Bohemians supporter dashed onto the field towards the Scottish substitutes. Police grabbed him and arrested him, but that one example was enough. Within minutes fans were scaling the protective fences around the playing pitch ready to do battle.

They fought with Bohemians fans . . . they stoned riot police who were called to quell the trouble. But even their shields and batons could not stop the trouble-makers. Nor could repeated appeals from Jock Wallace who went to the Rangers end of the ground to ask the fighting fans to behave.

Earlier, in the first half, Rangers' young goalkeeper Nicky Walker had had a golf ball hurled at him and Bohemians fans had burned a Union Jack on the terracings – an act designed to enrage the Rangers followers from Ulster.

At the end of the match the area surrounding the ground was sealed off by the special riot police as they tried to keep order. But a bitter and angry Jock Wallace admitted: 'What happened tonight was a disgrace. I was disgusted with the way some of our so-called supporters behaved. They went crazy. I was too scared about what was happening on the terracings to concentrate on the match itself.

'Twice I tried to get them to quieten down and behave. They wouldn't listen. We don't want them following this club. Anyone who wants to behave like this should stay away from Rangers games. That is my message to them.'

Wallace and his players left upset at the single goal defeat they suffered – but even more worried that they could be banned from Europe after just a single appearance!

Amazingly the club was saved because the official UEFA observer from Luxembourg did not see any of the major incidents. At that stage he was in the boardroom having a cup of tea. He said later: 'I did not see any of the trouble at half time.' That went into his report to the European Union, the soccer bosses of the Continent, and so Rangers were spared the kind of punishment they had feared most of all.

As to the game itself, it was a disappointing start to a new European beginning. Yet within seven minutes it had looked like being so different. Winger Davie Cooper, newly restored to the Scottish international side, went past two Irish defenders before chipping the ball so accurately into the middle. Young striker Ally McCoist was there, bustling in ahead of the Dublin defence, to guide a shot into the net. A dream opening for what was to become a nightmare!

Twenty-two-year-old Nicky Walker, making his European debut, had to contend with missiles being hurled at him from the terracings. That couldn't have helped his concentration and he was at fault for the goals Rangers eventually lost.

Striker Rocky O'Brien equalised in twenty-five minutes after the keeper failed to reach a pass back from centre half Craig Paterson. Even then, though, the situation scarcely looked crucial especially when Dave McPherson rose to reach a corner from Cooper and power his header out of reach of the Bohemians keeper Dermot O'Neil. Perhaps it was the ease with which they were able to score these two goals which made Rangers relax. Perhaps they thought that they could coast to the victory they wanted and that the pre-match warnings from their manager could be ignored.

Anyhow when O'Brien scored again ten minutes before half time Rangers never recovered. Again Nicky Walker was at fault, failing to hold a cross and then letting it fall at O'Brien's feet. He scrambled it into the net as the young keeper tried to recover.

Now, with the trouble on the terracings haunting them and their lead being wiped out twice, Rangers hit their worst form of the season. They slumped badly in the second half and even though Jock Wallace replaced his strike force of Sandy Clark and Ally McCoist with Iain Ferguson and John MacDonald they never looked like scoring again.

For Bohemians it was all so different. . . .

Just six minutes after half time they had taken the lead with the goal which was eventually to win them this first-leg tie. Their skipper, local postman Gino Lawless, sent in a snap shot from long range. Walker stood rooted to his line clearly believing the ball was going wide. Instead it bulged the net and had the £60-a-week part-time Irish players celebrating and then going on to look for even more goals against a Rangers team which was suddenly vulnerable. A defence which had lost just one goal in its previous six games had now lost three – and at the end of that tragic night they were happy to settle for being just one goal down with the second leg coming at Ibrox in two weeks time.

Boss Wallace was angry at the defeat. 'It was our first defeat of the season,' he growled, 'and it hurt. Part-time teams in a Cup tie can always cause problems. Airdrie knocked Aberdeen out of the Skol Cup and we should have had that in mind when we went on the field. I tried to tell the players that the game would be hard but it was harder than they expected.

'I'm not going to make excuses for the defeat. Sure the players were concerned about the trouble on the terracings but that is not why we lost. We didn't play well enough for the whole ninety minutes and we must make sure that we are in the right frame of mind for the return. That won't be easy either!'

How prophetic that remark was to prove! Even Jock Wallace could not have known how difficult the tie would be for Rangers, who had, by the time the game came round, made centre half Craig Paterson their new captain.

Again Wallace made it clear to the players and the public that he expected Bohemians to do more than simply make up the numbers for what so many thought might be a goal romp for the Scots.

He maintained at the pre-game training: 'We are not taking on a bunch of inexperienced laddies. Some of them have had more European experience than some of our lads. And they don't have a single player under twenty-four years of age in their side. They will be organized. They will drop back into a defensive formation to protect their goal lead and to drag us upfield so they can maybe cancel out at least one of the valuable away goals we scored over there. We know that and the fans will have to appreciate it and be patient.

'Our job is to reach the next round of the tournament – that is the most vital thing of all for us on the night.'

Thirty-one thousand people turned up at Ibrox to testify to the incredible drawing power of the Glasgow club; all drawn there to see their team play a team of Irish part-timers . . . but really there because even though the opposition was something less than glamorous this was still Europe. And that is where they believe their team belongs. . . .

But for long enough that belief was stretched to its limits as the Irishmen funneled neatly and compactly back into deep defence and Rangers tried and tried and tried again to find a way past them to settle the troublesome tie.

Indeed just before half time, veteran keeper Peter McCloy was almost struck by the jinx which had haunted Nicky Walker in Ireland. He allowed a shot from Bohemians midfielder Paul Doolin to slither through his legs but somehow recovered to stop the ball before it edged across the goal line. That and a reckless pass back from Dave McKinnon were all he was asked to deal with in the whole ninety minutes.

Bohemians, after all, were at Ibrox to protect the lead from the first leg, just as so many other teams had come to Ibrox in the past to do exactly the same thing. It was Rangers' one hundred and twenty-first tie in Europe – and for eight-four agonising minutes it seemed as if it would be their last one of that season.

That's how long it took them to level the aggregate score and to push themselves ahead on the rule in Europe which has away goals counting double. The Irishmen had frustrated most of their attacking attempts while twice, when they did get through to seriously threaten Dermot O'Neil's goal, luck went against them. Ian Redford and substitute striker Davie Mitchell both saw tries hit the woodwork and bounce clear as the huge Ibrox crowd willed the ball over the line.

There were just twenty or so Bohemians fans sitting on their own in a special area in one of the Ibrox stands – but they enjoyed so much of that night while the Rangers fans jeered their own team from the field at half time.

Whether the jeers helped, or whether it was a tongue lashing

Below left: This is the diving header from Ian Redford which clinched the game for Rangers. Bohemians' defence is shattered as Redford hurls himself horizontal to place the ball past keeper Dermot O'Neill (not in the picture)

Below right: Ian Redford turns away, arm raised, after the second goal for Rangers in their 2–0 win over Bohemians at Ibrox. Now, at this moment, Rangers know they are in the second round of UEFA Cup

from Jock Wallace which worked the miracle is anyone's guess. But how Rangers fought in that second half and ultimately Bohemians cracked under the strain. It all became too much for them as Rangers powered into one attack after another. As one wave was beaten back from the penalty box another took its place and the Irishmen wilted and then surrendered in those dramatic last minutes!

In eight-four minutes a Davie Cooper free kick beat the Irishmen who were crowded into their own penalty area. Rangers' skipper Craig Paterson, upfield to help his team towards victory in their late attacks, got to the ball and rammed a header beyond the Bohemians keeper Dermot O'Neil.

That was it. Rangers were through to the second round of the tournament and the cheers which roared round the stadium were as much of relief as of celebration.

Then, before the end – in fact it was in the very last seconds of the game – Ian Redford followed his captain's example. Another free kick from Cooper, another header and this time the Rangers fans were celebrating. The jeers which had met the team at half time had disappeared. In their place came the familiar tunes of glory which had echoed around Ibrox on so many other European nights – most of them so much more glamorous than this one.

But it wasn't glamour which counted. All that counted now was that Rangers were in the next round. The team would be given another chance in the UEFA Cup tournament. Jock Wallace would have another taste of Europe and the fans might, this time around, see some of the game's greats.

So Bohemians headed back for Dublin after becoming the one hundred and twenty-first statistic in Rangers' long European history. Meantime Rangers and their fans waited to see what the draw would bring.

They had missed the sense of the European big time in that first round. Now they wanted to see the stars and their wish was granted when the draw was made in Switzerland. For Rangers were drawn to meet mighty Inter Milan of Italy.

This was to be the *real* test for Jock Wallace's Rangers team. And everyone at Ibrox knew that.